JAPAN

From the Source

*Authentic recipes from the
people that know them best*

Written by Tienlon Ho, Rebecca Milner and Ippo Nakahara
Photographed by Junichi Miyazaki

CONTENTS

INTRODUCTION

Ramen noodles, miso, sashimi. It would be easy to assume that Japanese cuisine is all about food.

But no. Or at least, it's not *just* about the food. The cuisine of this teeming archipelago of 3000 islands is a living part of its culture. And much like the fibre of the Japanese soul, it has been shaped by the nation's history, and not least by the rise, over a millennium ago, of Japanese Buddhism.

The sushi we know and love today owes its creation to the rise of the religion – the popularity of early sushi proliferated after emperors banned the eating of meat. The dish, as with Japanese laws, has greatly evolved since then. The first sushi was not even eaten with rice; instead it was simply a meal of fish that had been preserved in the fermenting grains.

In Japan it's believed that food should be devoured with all five senses: not just smell, taste and sight, but also touch (the texture of ingredients, the smooth warmth of bamboo chopsticks), and even sound (a high-end *ryotei* is oddly quiet, the better to appreciate the experience of eating).

Like rice, which originally came from China, the introduction of the Five Elements Philosophy has shaped Japanese cuisine for centuries. Focusing on earth, wood, fire, water and metal, the philosophy rests on the principle that each element must be balanced against each of the others, in order for the world and everything in it to maintain its equilibrium.

Put simply, each type of ingredient relates to one of the five elements by its taste and colour: sweet and yellow, orange or brown to earth; sour and green to wood; bitter and red to fire; salty and black, blue or purple to water; and spicy and white to metal. Even cooking techniques link to one of the five elements: boiling, steaming and poaching to water, for example, and smoking to wood.

Any Japanese meal – from simple home-cooked fare to the most structured, formal *kaiseki* – aims to blend each of these elements for balance and nutrition. Unsurprisingly, this provides myriad benefits for our health, as does the act of lingering over our food and cherishing each mouthful with all our senses – the latter has been proven to aid digestion and portion control. It's clear that meals taken the traditional Japanese way are good for us. That they are such a pleasure to consume, too? Well, that's just a happy coincidence.

COOK'S NOTES

This book aims to deliver Japan's best local dishes – direct from the kitchens where they've been perfected and practised for decades or generations. Authenticity is at the heart of every dish we feature.

That means that some ingredients may be difficult to find in general stores. Most should be available in Asian supermarkets or online but, where possible, we have suggested more easily sourced substitutes, too. The glossary on page 268 will help to identify unfamiliar ingredients.

In the spirit of authenticity, we have retained the chefs' original methods in these recipes, but have always tried where possible to offer alternatives, to help you produces these dishes when time is pressed or specialist equipment not available.

For basic recipes for rice and dashi, see pages 264–5.

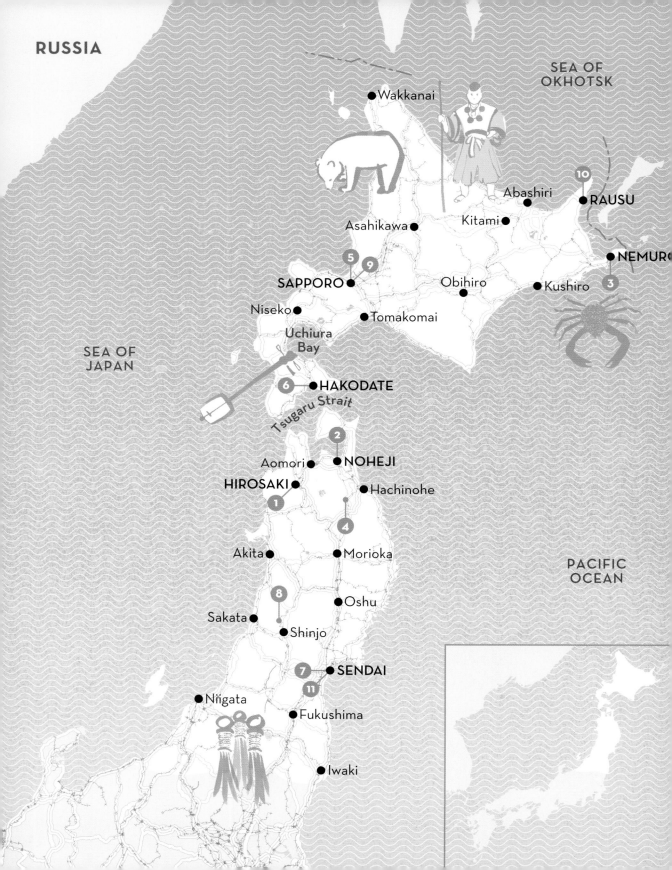

RUSSIA

SEA OF
OKHOTSK

Wakkanai

Abashiri

10

Kitami

RAUSU

Asahikawa

NEMURO

5 **9**

SAPPORO

Obihiro

Kushiro

3

Niseko

Tomakomai

Uchiura
Bay

SEA OF
JAPAN

6 **HAKODATE**

Tsugaru Strait

2

Aomori

NOHEJI

HIROSAKI

Hachinohe

1

4

Akita

Morioka

PACIFIC
OCEAN

8

Oshu

Sakata

Shinjo

7 **SENDAI**

11

Niigata

Fukushima

Iwaki

NORTHERN JAPAN

Stews and soups are popular in these cooler climes, along with local seafood specialities, such as salmon and crab in Hokkaido

IGA-MENCHI
Squid croquettes

These crisp-fried croquettes of juicy squid, sweet onion and vegetables are a staple in the northern Tohoku city of Hirosaki. The Tsugaru Akatsuki Club members champion homemade.

Iga means squid in the Tsugaru dialect of western Aomori. The local variety, Pacific flying squid – yes it really can propel itself up and over the water – comes from the Tsugaru Strait, the freezing stretch of water that separates Tohoku, the northernmost part of mainland Japan, from the more-northern-still island of Hokkaido. Hirosaki, an old castle city on the Tsugaru plains, is 50km south of the strait. 'In the old days, squid was a real luxury and we only served it for company. Now it's a one-hour drive to the port, but before cars it was a day in a horse and carriage,' explains Samago Kudo, the leader of the Tsugaru Akatsuki Club.

The Tsugaru Akatsuki Club members are active in preserving and gathering traditional recipes from the Tsugaru region of Aomori. All of the members belong to farming families. Kudo, now 75, founded the group 20 years ago, prompted by the desire to preserve the knowledge and traditions of the older generations, those who could remember the days before cars and refrigerators.

Iga-menchi is one of those dishes originally designed to stretch a precious source of protein. The main body of the squid, the tender, almost creamy part, was served as a sashimi dish and the tougher bits (the legs and ears) were minced for use in iga-menchi. As squid is now readily available, the whole thing is often used in the dish. Vegetables like onions, carrots and cabbage are commonly added – although every household has a slightly different way of serving it depending on what they grow. Iga-menchi can be served plain, with soy sauce, or tonkatsu sauce for dipping, and as Kudo says, 'It's an excellent snack to accompany sake.'

Chef //
Sumago Kudo
Location //
Tsugaru Akatsuki
Club, Aomori

IGA-MENCHI
Squid croquettes

Serves 5

Preparation time: 30 mins
Cooking time: 30 mins

300g (10½ oz) squid
¼ head of cabbage (about 200g/7 oz),
*   finely shredded*
2 small onions or 1 large, finely diced
50g (1¾ oz) carrot, finely diced
1 medium egg
80g (2¾ oz) flour
5g (¼ oz) katakuriko (potato starch)
1 tbsp sake
cooking oil, for frying
salt and pepper

1 Rinse the squid under cold running water and remove the insides, eyes and beak. Use a sharp knife to dice the squid into 5mm (¼ in) pieces. Then using the cutting edge of the knife, pound the squid repeatedly for several minutes – this will tenderise the pieces.

2 Rinse the cabbage and place in a strainer lined with paper towels. Squeeze out any excess water. Transfer the cabbage in a large bowl with the squid, onions and carrots, then crack in the egg. Add the flour and katakuriko, and season generously with salt and pepper. Mix thoroughly with a wooden spoon, then add the sake and set aside while you heat up the pan.

3 Add enough oil to a large frying pan to come 1cm (½ in) up the side and set over high heat until almost smoking. Test whether the oil is hot enough by adding a drop of batter – it should sizzle when it hits the oil.

4 Carefully add generous spoonfuls of the mixture into the hot oil, in batches of four or five – stand back as they will spit – and shallow fry for 4–5 minutes until the edges of each croquette are crisp and golden. Flip over and fry for a further 2 minutes, until cooked through. Serve immediately.

'What they serve in restaurants isn't good.
They skimp on the squid and add too much
flour. Homemade is better.'

HOTATE MISO KAI-YAKI
Scallops simmered in miso

This is a fortifying, easy-to-make – and decadent – dish. People come from all over to eat the scallops at Matsuura Shokudo, simmered with miso and egg, and served in their shells.

Matsuura Shokudo is a small diner that may seem unassuming from the outside, but it is the best place to eat in Aomori. Boasting an unusually long history of 125 years, Keisuke Matsuura's grandparents first opened the restaurant in 1891, the year the railroad arrived in Noheji. Back then, Noheji was a busy port town. Trade had brought wealth and cosmopolitan ideas, and the town flourished, offering food more sophisticated than elsewhere in the north. Noheji's glory days are now gone, but the thing the town still has going for it is its scallops. They are considered the best in Japan. There isn't really any reason to come to Noheji other than to eat scallops at Matsuura Shokudo (and people do come for that reason).

Food in Aomori is intensely local; in Noheji they make miso kai-yaki with scallops. Just up the coast in Mutsu, they make it with squid. Keisuke's wife, Ritsu Matsuura, explains that the dish was traditionally served to women after childbirth as a restorative and, considering it's a bit of a luxury, a kind of 'push present'. She adds, laughing: 'Actually we call it miso "ka-yaki" here. We tend to slur our words because it's too cold to open your mouth all the way.' Noheji has a cold climate and this is all the better for the scallops, which are plump, firm and just a bit sweet. Combined with savoury miso and creamy egg – plus an umami kick from the katsuobushi – they're a rich treat.

Keisuke and Ritsu do everything at the restaurant themselves. Their long day starts at 4.30am. Before beginning preparation for the lunch service, they put in a few hours' work on their fields, which supply the diner with burdock and spring onions. It's not an easy life for a couple in their 80s, but, says Ritsu, 'I enjoy it.'

Chef //
Ritsu and Keisuke Matsuura
Location //
Matsuura Shokudo, Aomori

HOTATE MISO KAI-YAKI
Scallops simmered in miso

Serves 4

Preparation time: 15 mins
Cooking time: 20 mins

4 medium-sized sushi-grade scallops with
their shells (about 200g/7oz)
100ml (3½fl oz) water
1 tbsp katsuobushi (dried bonito flakes), finely
shaved if available (see tip below)
1 tbsp sugar
1 heaped tbsp miso paste
4 medium eggs, beaten
2 chives, diagonally sliced into 1.5cm
(¾ in) lengths

Tip

*For this dish, it's best to use finely shaved
katsuobushi (dried bonito flakes), which
are often used as a garnish. If shaved
is unavailable, simply microwave the
katsuobushi for 10 seconds and break up
the larger flakes into small pieces.*

*If sushi-grade scallops are not available,
use ordinary fresh scallops but cook them
through completely.*

1   If using scallops in the shell, shuck them. To do this, hold a scallop in one hand with the thick-ridged side of the shell facing upwards. Use a flat metal spatula to loosen the scallop from the shell and carefully prise open. Remove the scallop and discard everything except the big abductor muscle. Set the shells aside. Rinse the scallop under cold running water and slice into domino-sized pieces.

2   Pour the water into a small saucepan, add the katsuobushi and bring to the boil. Add the sugar and miso, stirring to dissolve.

3   Turn off heat and add about two-thirds of the beaten eggs, the scallops and chives, and mix until well combined.

4   Lay a piece of sturdy wire mesh directly over an open-flame hob and place the saucepan on top (this will protect the stovetop and make it easier to cook in the shells later). Turn the hob to low heat, and stir the mixture for 2–3 minutes, until the eggs set and the scallops are about half-cooked (they will start to look opaque). Remove from the heat.

5   Next, on a plate, lay the reserved scallop shells. Divide the scallop mixture from the pan between the shells. Carefully lift one shell and place on the mesh-wired stovetop (or two if they will fit). (Alternatively, do this on a barbecue.) Spoon over some of the remaining beaten eggs and use chopsticks to evenly distribute. Cook for about 2 minutes over medium heat, or until the eggs are just set.

6   Use two metal tongs to remove the shells and arrange on a heatproof dish while you continue to cook the remaining shells, scallops and egg mixture. Serve immediately.

TEPPO-JIRU
Miso soup with crab

Miso soup is always the bridesmaid, never the bride. The exception is found at Suzuki Shokudo. A whole crab in every bowl, the soup is the star of the show.

Chef //
Endo Kazunori and
Kawakami Noriko
Location //
Suzuki Shokudo,
Nemuro, Hokkaido

Teppo-jiru is a curious name: it means 'rifle soup'. Endo Kazunori of Suzuki Shokudo says this is because 'when you eat the crab legs, it looks like you're cleaning a rifle,' as he mimes the high-concentration needed to fish out crabmeat with a long-stemmed fork. Endo has been running Suzuki Shokudo for seven years, after his aunt, the original owner, passed away. 'It would have been a shame if everything she created were just to vanish,' he says of the decision to give up the life of a fisherman for a more sedentary one in a restaurant. And Suzuki Shokudo is something of a landmark, if only in that roadside kitsch sort of way: it is Japan's Eastern-most diner. You can look out the windows and see the Kuril Islands, just a few kilometres offshore, that belong to Russia. It is also a beacon for motorcyclists, who come to stay in the diner's 'rider house' – a simple, dirt-cheap accommodation for travellers on two wheels.

Then there's the soup: teppo-jiru is a Nemuro speciality. Crabs are fished all over Hokkaido, but only Nemuro has hanasaki (also known as king) crabs. *Hanasaki* means 'blooming flower' – a reference to the bright red hue of the crabs when cooked. They are meaty and spiky, and have short fat legs, which fit perfectly in a bowl of soup. 'Teppo-jiru is often made with only the legs. But I like to make it with the whole crab,' says Endo. This is because the *kani-miso* (crab guts), which are prized in Japanese cooking for their rich, salty crabbiness, adds richness and depth of flavour to the soup. This dish uses frozen crab, which means the crab season can be extended beyond the usual two-month window in summer. 'You have to break it open,' he says, getting ready to demonstrate with a huge meat cleaver, 'and if it's not frozen, the crab will explode.'

TEPPO-JIRU
Miso soup with crab

Serves 2

Preparation time: 10 mins
Cooking time: 15 mins

2 medium-sized frozen hanasaki (king) crabs
   (about 800g (1¾lb) each)
4 tbsp miso paste, or more to taste
1 chive, finely chopped, to serve

1 First prepare the crabs by breaking off the legs and cutting the tips from each leg. Place them, belly up, on a sturdy chopping board. Wedge a sharp, heavy cleaver into the middle of each of the crabs, lengthwise, and place your other hand on top of the knife. Firmly press down on the knife and crab, up and down, to cut the crab in half.

2 Rinse the crab under cold running water and place in a large saucepan with enough water to cover. Bring to a boil and cook, covered, for 5 minutes over high heat.

3 Lower the heat. Add a ladleful of crab broth to a mug or small bowl and whisk in the miso paste to dissolve completely. Return the mixture to the pan and simmer briefly. Add more miso to taste if necessary.

4 Divide the crabs between two bowls and ladle the soup broth over the top. Sprinkle with chives and serve immediately. Drink the soup first, while it's still piping hot.

Know your miso

Miso is a salty paste made of fermented soybeans. The most common kind is shiro-miso ('white' miso, though the colour is usually golden or light brown) made from boiled soybeans and rice. Lighter and sweeter than other varieties, white miso is the most versatile and therefore the go-to miso for most recipes. Aka-miso ('red' miso), darker in colour and deeper in flavour, is made from steamed soybeans, less rice and aged for over a year. It can be used to make a particularly pungent miso soup, but is more commonly used in bastes and marinades. Rich, earthy hatcho miso is made purely from soybeans and aged over two years. Hatcho miso is the signature miso of the Nagoya area. In Japan, it is perfectly acceptable to custom mix your own to make chogo-miso, 'blended' miso.

HITTSUMI
Hand-pulled noodle soup

Hittsumi, hand-pulled noodles in a woody broth, is perfect comfort food. Noriko Kudo learned how to make this dish from her mother, who learned how to make it from her mother.

Rice may be synonymous with Japanese cuisine, but it doesn't grow plentifully everywhere. The drier, rugged terrain of Sannohe is better suited to wheat, the key ingredient in hittsumi. The name for the dish comes from the word 'to pinch' in the local dialect, which describes how the noodles are made – pinching and pulling the dough. The irregular shapes that result, which look somewhat like stretched earlobes, give the dish a rough-hewn quality. Made correctly, they have the heft and bite of dumplings. The broth is steeped in the flavours of land and sea: shiitake, burdock root and carrots; kombu, katsuobushi and niboshi.

This soup is served on cold wintery evenings in homes around Iwate and southeast Aomori. 'It's an old recipe. One for scarce times, but one that anyone can make,' says Noriko Kudo. Kudo is the head of a collective of local women, all from farming families, who cook and serve hittsumi (along with other local dishes) at the San Sun farmers market. She and her friends started the roadside market 20 years ago as a place to sell their produce to passing motorists. It has since expanded to become the hub of community life in Sannohe, a gathering spot and the site of local festivals. While Kudo enjoys introducing travellers to the foods she grew up with, it's the community element at the market that she treasures most. Most of the members are, like Kudo, now in their 70s. The San Sun kitchen is full of gossip and laughter as members chop vegetables, stir giant pots of broth, and knead the stiff dough for the hittsumi with their feet – a long-time local tradition.

Hittsumi is deceptively filling: serve it as the women of San Sun do, with a tofu dish, some pickles on the side and a hot mugwort tea.

Chef //
Noriko Kudo
Location //
San Sun Chokubai
Hiroba, Sannohe

HITTSUMI
Hand-pulled noodle soup

Serves 4

Preparation time: 20 mins
Cooking time: 2 hrs plus overnight resting

For the noodles
500g (1lb 2 oz) flour
1 tsp salt
250ml (7½ fl oz) cold water

For the broth
75g (2¾ oz) carrot, halved
50g (1¾ oz) burdock root, halved
10g (¼ oz) shiitake mushrooms, cleaned
  and stems removed
30g (1 oz) niboshi (dried baby sardines)
2.5g (¹⁄₁₀ oz) kombu
12g (½ oz) katsuobushi (dried bonito flakes)
2 litres (68 fl oz) water
100ml (3½ fl oz) soy sauce
50ml (1¾ fl oz) cooking sake
scant 2 tbsp mirin
1 spring onion (scallion), finely sliced
salt and pepper

Niboshi
(dried baby sardines)

Added to stock, niboshi impart an umami depth of flavour and pleasant bitterness if used in large enough quantities. Once opened, they can be stored in the fridge for up to a month (or frozen for up to three).

---

1 First, make the dough. Put the flour in a large bowl and add the water gradually, stirring as you do so with a wooden spoon, until it comes together into a dough. Use your hands, if needed.

2 If you want to knead it the traditional way, put the dough in a plastic bag inside a paper bag and place on the floor. Use your feet and a gentle stepping motion to knead the dough for a few minutes. Then fold the dough into quarters and repeat three times. Sprinkle the dough with flour as necessary to keep it from sticking to the bag. Alternatively, knead for a few minutes on a lightly dusted surface with your hands until the dough is elastic.

3 Set dough aside (wrapped in plastic bag) overnight at room temperature.

4 The next day, cut the dough into four pieces and form into balls about 10cm (4 in) diameter. Fill a large bowl with ice-cold water and set a colander on top. Set aside.

5 Bring a large pan of water to the boil. Cut one dough ball into thirds, lengthways. Holding one strip of dough in one hand, use your other hand to press and pull the dough, pulling off chunks the size of dominos (they will look more like dumplings than noodles) and tossing them into the boiling water. Cook for about 3 minutes, or until they float to the surface of the water. Use a slotted spoon to scoop the dumplings out of the water and then transfer them to the colander set over the bowl of cold water. Repeat the hand-pulling and cooking with the remaining dough.

6 To make the broth, put the carrot, burdock root, shiitake, niboshi and kombu in a large saucepan. Pour in the water and bring to the boil over high heat.

7 Put the katsuobushi in a muslin (cheesecloth) bag. When the water comes to the boil, add the katsuobushi, reduce the heat to medium-low and simmer, covered, for 1 hour.

8 Use a slotted spoon to remove and discard the kombu, katsuobushi and niboshi. Remove and plunge the carrot, burdock root, and shiitake under cold running water to cool quickly. Drain and slice the vegetables into fine matchsticks and set aside.

9 Add the soy sauce, sake and mirin to the broth and season to taste. Drop the dumplings into the broth and bring to a boil. Immediately turn off the heat and ladle the soup and dumplings into large bowls. Serve topped with the sliced vegetables and spring onion.

MISO RAMEN
Noodle soup

The infinite varieties of ramen and today's cultish obsession with them began humbly with the dish's introduction to Japan in the 19th century. Sapporo's is a rich, opaque, miso-flavoured ramen.

Getting a ramen chef to share his or her recipe is no easy feat: house secrets are notoriously guarded. Menya Saimi, known for their creamy, perfectly balanced bowl of noodles, is a favourite among local ramen critics (yes, they exist). That Oku Masuhiko of Menya Saimi was willing to open up his kitchen suggests either extreme confidence or recklessness. (He's also sentimental: the shop name includes a Chinese character from each of his daughters' names.) 'The secret is that most shops are doing pretty much the same thing. Just tweaking things here and there,' says Oku, in a hoodie and plastic sandals, stirring an enormous pot of broth that has been bubbling since 5am. What's Oku's special trick? 'Well, I put a little bit of grated ginger on top,' he says. That can't possibly be it: Menya Saimi's ramen is smooth and mellow, bold-tasting but not overpowering, with dense, curly noodles and an array of toppings that include chashu pork, seasoned bamboo shoots and bean sprouts. He shrugs.

Oku trained for seven years at another landmark noodle shop, Sumire, which is responsible for popularising what is now considered Sapporo's signature ramen style. Miso ramen starts with an oily broth – in Saimi's case one made from pork bones – which is seasoned with salty miso. It falls heavily on the *kotteri* side, the word used to describe rich, opaque soup. 'The vegetables that garnish the top are stir-fried first; this is key for Sapporo-style ramen,' says Oku. It's a combination that feels just about right for the city's long, cold winters. Ramen may be categorised as comfort food or late night drinking food, but it is still a complex dish. At each stage in the process different smells bubble up from Saimi's kitchen: the strong funk of boiling pig bones, the piercing aroma of garlic sizzling in hot oil, and the toasty, nutty fragrance of sautéing miso. It's the latter that welcomes customers, who can be found lining up outside when the doors open at 10.45am.

Chef //
Oku Masuhiko
Location //
Menya Saimi,
Sapporo, Hokkaido

MISO RAMEN
Noodle soup

Serves 5

Preparation time: 1 hr
Cooking time: 7 hrs (with downtime)

A note on timing: homemade ramen is an
all-day commitment. Here's a rough timeline for
getting it on the table at 7pm:
Noon: start preparing the stock
4pm: prepare the chashu pork
6pm: remove the chashu pork from stock and add
it to the marinade
6:30pm: prepare your toppings

For the tonkotsu (pork bone) broth
500g (1 lb 2 oz) pork leg bones
18 litres (4.5 gal) water
5g ($^7/_8$ oz) niboshi (dried baby sardines)
   (see note, page 26)
15g (½ oz) chicken feet, skinned removed and
   minced (ground)
3 spring onions (scallions), green parts only

For the chashu pork
1 kg (2 lb 3 oz) pork shoulder
900ml (30½ fl oz) soy sauce
100g (3½ oz) sugar
7.5cm (13 in) piece kombu
6 dried red Japanese peppers or 3 dried chillies
1 tbsp cooking oil

Tip

Store the leftover chashu marinade in
a jar in the fridge for up to 1 week
and use it to flavour Shoyu Ramen
instead of the miso.

---

1 Start by making the tonkotsu broth. Trim the
pork shoulder for the chashu pork of the excess
fat and reserve, set the shoulder aside. Place the
pork bones for the broth in a large stockpot and
fill with plenty of water. Bring to a rapid boil over
high heat, drain and rinse thoroughly to remove
any remaining blood. This step will result in a
clearer, more refined broth.

2 Place the rinsed bones in a clean stockpot, add
the water and bring to a boil. Cook uncovered
over low heat for 4 hours, skimming any foam
that rises to the surface and stirring occasionally.
Expect the stock to boil down considerably.

3 Put the niboshi in a muslin (cheesecloth) bag and
add to the pan along with the minced chicken
feet, spring onions and, if using, the reserved
pork fat from the pork shoulder. Continue to
cook for another 2 hours while you prepare the
chashu pork.

4 For the chashu pork, combine all the
ingredients except the pork shoulder and oil in
a large saucepan. Bring to a boil and simmer
over low heat for 2 hours – this is your
marinade. Remove from the heat and allow to
cool to room temperature.

5 Meanwhile, roll the pork shoulder firmly and tie
with kitchen string at 1cm (½ in) intervals. Heat
the oil in a large pan over medium-high heat and
brown the pork all over. Transfer the pork to the
tonkotsu broth and simmer for 1½ hours.

6 Remove the pork from the broth and add it to
the now-cooled marinade. Allow it to soak for 30
minutes for the flavours to mingle. Remove and
set aside.

For the toppings

cooking oil, for stir-frying
100g (3½ oz) jarred seasoned bamboo
  shoots (such as Momoya), drained
75g (2¾ oz) finely chopped garlic
250g (9 oz) bean sprouts
85g (3 oz) lard
25g (1 oz) minced (ground) lean pork
ichimi red pepper seasoning, to taste
sansho pepper, to taste
50g (1¾ oz) onions, thinly sliced
300g (10½ oz) miso paste
3 spring onions (scallions), finely sliced,
  to serve
750g (1 lb 11 oz) egg noodles
4cm (1½ in) piece of ginger, peeled
  and grated

7 Next, start on the toppings. In a wok or large wide pan, heat the oil over high heat and stir-fry the bamboo for 2–3 minutes. Remove and set aside. Add a little more oil and stir-fry one-third of the finely chopped garlic until fragrant, then add the bean sprouts and cook for 2–3 minutes. Ladle in a bit of the simmering broth, cover the pan and steam the sprouts briefly. Turn off the heat and set aside.

8 When just about ready to serve, melt the lard in a wok over high heat. Add the remaining garlic, stir until fragrant, then add the minced pork. Stir a few times then add the miso and mix well. Sprinkle over the red pepper and sansho pepper to taste. Add the onions and stir-fry for about 3 minutes. Immediately turn off heat, then add the contents of the pan to the broth, stirring gently.

9 Bring a large pan of water to the boil and cook the noodles according to the packet instructions. Drain and divide between serving bowls.

10 Slice half the chashu pork into 5mm (¼in) slices and dice the rest. Using a blowtorch, sear the slices of pork until golden brown (alternatively, place under a hot grill). Place in a bowl and add the grated ginger.

11 To serve, bring the broth to the boil, just to reheat, then remove from the heat. Ladle the broth over the noodles into each bowl. Arrange the bamboo, bean sprouts, chashu pork and spring onions in an artful mound in the centre of each bowl. Serve immediately.

It's all in the sauce

In many ways it is the tare (sauce) that is the DNA of a restaurant. Recipes are closely guarded, yet even still it would be nearly impossible to replicate. Tare is a living thing, like a sourdough starter: it is fed, new ingredients are blended together with the aged ingredients, which have accumulated years of bits of whatever grilled meat has been dipped in it. One of the most touching gifts a chef can give to an apprentice, before he or she starts out on his own, is some tare. Without a well-developed sauce, there's no way to appear anything but green. All tare recipes in this book are merely a starting point: feel free to play around and develop your own signature sauce.

HAKODATE TOMOEGATA KAISEN-DON
Hakodate seafood rice bowl

The Hakodate morning market draws hungry visitors who come to sample Hokkaido's famous seafood. Here you'll find Kikuyo Shokudo, a diner selling mouthwatering kaisen-don, lightly seasoned raw seafood on rice.

The Hakodate morning market, several tightly wound blocks next to Hakodate Harbour, comes to life just before dawn. Workers in rubber boots and woolly hats put out styrofoam crates of sea urchin, salmon roe and squid from Hokkaido's chilly waters. Grills are lit for scallops and crabs, luring the first sleepy-eyed visitors to the market with the promise of a fresh seafood breakfast. When Kikuyo Shokudo opened 60 years ago, it was a ten-stool counter joint selling breakfast to market workers. Since then, it has expanded to make room for a heavy rotation of visitors. It has also inspired many imitators, though none can rival Kikuyo's attention to detail: the salmon roe is seasoned daily in-house and rice is cooked with a made-to-order clay steamer heated by charcoal briquettes.

The diner's signature dish is Hakodate tomoegata kaisen-don, which makes use of three of Hakodate's most sought after delicacies: sea urchin, salmon roe and scallops. The word *tomoegata* refers to the tri-part pattern of the ingredients. Really though, kaisen-don can be made with any combination of ingredients arranged in any pattern. In general, there is little guidance when it comes to kaisen-don, other than to eat it immediately. The dish calls for creativity: 'Use whatever you like!' says Nakamura Yasunori, the son-in-law of the original Kikuyo. These days, Nakamura and his wife run the shop together.

Unlike sushi, kaisen-don uses unseasoned rice. More often than not it's served at a diner attached to a fishmonger or market, ensuring fresh fish is always on hand. While this dish may hardly seem like cooking, there are subtle ways to enhance the flavour of the ingredients, such as marinating the roe in soy sauce and sake, or seasoning the sea urchin with wasabi-spiked soy sauce. At Kikuyo, kaisen-don is served with miso soup flecked with rock seaweed – another Hokkaido speciality.

Chef //
Nakamura Yasunori
Location //
Kikuyo Shokudo, Hokkaido

HAKODATE TOMOEGATA KAISEN-DON

Hakodate seafood rice bowl

Serves 4

Preparation time: 10 mins plus overnight for marinating unseasoned salmon roe
Cooking time: 30 mins, plus rice cooking time

300g (10½ oz) salmon roe (see tip)
1 tbsp sake
2 tbsp soy sauce, plus extra for drizzling
600g (1lb 5oz) white rice
250g (9 oz) sea urchin
250g (9 oz) sashimi-grade scallops
dried nori, shredded

For the wasabi-soy sauce
2 tbsp basic dashi (see page 265)
1 tbsp soy sauce
2½ tsp grated fresh wasabi, or to taste

Tip

In Japan, the salmon roe in the supermarket is sold pre-seasoned (often with MSG and preservatives). For this recipe, ideally you want fresh salmon roe, unseasoned, from a fishmonger.

1 In a bowl, combine the salmon roe with the sake and 2 tablespoons soy sauce. Leave to marinate overnight in the fridge.

2 The next day, cook the rice following the instructions on page 264. Allow to cool slightly for 5 minutes – it should still be warm.

3 Meanwhile, make the wasabi-soy sauce by combining the dashi and soy sauce with grated wasabi to taste.

4 Divide rice between large serving bowls and slightly smooth the surface without pressing or compacting the rice. Add a spoonful of the seasoned salmon roe arranging it in a wedge-shape on top of the rice in each bowl. Using chopsticks if you wish, carefully arrange the sea urchin in another wedge.

5 Lastly, slice the scallops lengthways into four pieces and place on top of the rice. Drizzle the wasabi-soy sauce over the sea urchin and the plain soy sauce over the scallops. Sprinkle dried nori and serve immediately.

Rice and side dishes

To say that rice (o-kome) is central to Japanese cooking is an understatement. While a small bowl of rice may come at the end of a kaiseki (haute cuisine) course, on the dining room table at home it is often the main dish. Accompanying the rice are the o-kazu (side dishes), made with a variety of meat, fish, tofu and vegetables for a balanced meal. If you walk down the shotengai (high street) in any residential neighbourhood, you'll see small shops selling takeaway o-kazu, maybe some panko-fried minced (ground) meat patties or aubergine simmered with miso. The rice, however, would have been made fresh at home with an electric rice cooker, the one kitchen appliance that Japanese people simply can't live without.

GYUTAN

*Barbecued beef tongue
with beef tail soup*

*Thin-slices of
charcoal-grilled
gyutan – beef
tongue –
have become
synonymous
with Sendai,
Tohoku's largest
city. Family-run
Umami Tasuke,
in business since
1948, was the first
place to serve it.*

Sendai's most famous dish was born in the competitive world of market food stalls. Keichiro Sano, a market vendor, was keen to coin a new dish that would be so complicated his neighbours wouldn't copy it. During a chance visit to one of the then-rare Western-style restaurants in the city he thought he'd found it – tongue stew. Sano learned how to make it, but ultimately decided that the demi-glace sauce in the stew wasn't worth the trouble. Instead of abandoning tongue altogether, he experimented with various cooking methods until he alighted on what has become the quintessential way to prepare tongue in Japan: saucer-thin medallions, generously salted and grilled over charcoal. The result is unlike anything you'd expect – melt-in-your-mouth tender medallions with a bacon-like crispness around the edges.

Ultimately, Sano was defeated: gyutan caught on in a big way and Umami Tasuke inspired a string of copycats. Today, there are dozens of restaurants in Sendai that specialise in it. When Sano passed away, his son Hatsuo, who trained at his father's side, took over. The elder Sano was a strict teacher: 'He used to weigh the skin I'd removed from the tongue to make sure I wasn't taking off too much,' recalls Hatsuo, who is now 72. But he is thankful to have been able to carry on the tradition of his father's cooking: 'When the old-timers, the guys in their 90s, come in and they tell me the taste hasn't changed, that it still tastes just like my father's cooking – that's the best compliment anyone could give me,' he says. Hatsuo's own son is waiting in the wings.

At Umami Tasuke, gyutan is served for lunch and dinner, as part of a set meal that includes beef tail soup, and rice cooked with barley and *nozawana* (rape leaf) pickles.

Chef //
Hatsuo Sano
Location //
Umami Tasuke, Sendai

GYUTAN
Barbecued beef tongue with beef tail soup

Serves 5

*Preparation time: 30 mins plus overnight
    marinating*
Cooking time: 5–6 hrs

For the beef
*750g (1lb 11oz) beef tongue (about 1 tongue), sliced
    into 4mm (¼in) thick slices (ask your butcher to
    do this and separate the tougher parts from the
    tip of the tongue)*
salt and pepper

For the beef tail soup
*500g (4½ pints) beef tail, cut into
    3cm (1¼in) chunks*
2.5 litres (85 fl oz) water
*2 spring onions (scallions), sliced finely
    on a diagonal*

1 Prepare the beef by selecting only the white-speckled pieces of tongue. Reserve the remaining tough pieces from the tip of the tongue for later. Take a sharp knife and score the white-speckled tongue slices on both sides, widthways, about 1cm (½ in) apart.

2 Sprinkle a plate generously with salt and arrange the slices of beef in a single layer on top. Generously season with salt and pepper. Add another layer of beef, season, and repeat until all the slices are on the plate. Cover and let sit overnight in the fridge.

3 The next day, make the soup. Bring plenty of water to boil in a large saucepan. Add the beef tail and blanch for 10 minutes. Drain and rinse the tail thoroughly under cold running water, until the water runs clear (this can take up to 20 minutes and will ensure a clean, clear soup).

4 Return the beef tail to the pan along with the reserved tongue tip, and add the 2.5 litres (85 fl oz) water. Bring to the boil and simmer over the lowest heat possible for 5–6 hours.

5 When you are about 30 minutes away from serving, remove the beef from fridge and let it come to room temperature.

6 Preheat a barbecue, grill (broiler) or yaki-ami (see tip, left) and cook the beef tongue for about 2–3 minutes per side, or until the edges turn golden and begin to crisp. Keep warm.

7 Season the soup with salt and pepper to taste. Add the spring onions and simmer for a couple of minutes to soften. Ladle the soup into bowls and serve with the gyutan.

Tip

*Gyutan can easily be served on its own,
and it's great for the barbecue. If you
want to make it inside on the stovetop,
try to get your hands on a yaki-ami, a
Japanese mesh metal griddle designed for
reproducing yaki (grilled) dishes at home.*

IMO-NI
Taro stew

Yamagata is famous for mountains and taro. The two are joined every autumn, when local communities head outdoors for imo-ni parties, sharing communal pots of stew amid soaring peaks.

Haruki Sato didn't set out to be a taro farmer. During his 20s, when he didn't know what he wanted to do, he was hanging out in his home town – a rural community of 8,000 people in Yamagata – helping his elderly grandparents with their farm. It was then that he discovered his grandmother had a few sacks of ancient seeds stashed away. These seeds turned out to be an heirloom variety of taro, called *jingoemon imo*, farmed during medieval times, which made sense, since Sato's family had been farming the same land for 20 generations. It was then that he decided he would take over his grandparents' farm and bring the long lost jingoemon imo back to life.

Sato and his wife bought a 150-year-old farmhouse, which they run as an informal bed and breakfast for friends and friends of friends. Every autumn, they host a cookout and make a big pot of taro stew, imo-ni. Parties of this sort are a Yamagata tradition during the harvest season, when the temperature drops to the point where a piping hot bowl of stew hits the right spot. Family and friends gather alongside streams to celebrate another season done and dusted.

Imo-ni is a classic home-cooked dish in Yamagata – you won't find it on the menu at restaurants. Each house has its own recipe and there are regional variations too, though in most cases it consists of taro, konnyaku and finely sliced beef simmered in soy sauce. Sato learned how to make this from his grandmother, whose recipe calls for the addition of mushrooms that grow abundantly in the woods around the family farm. In Japan, taro is loved for being *nuru nuru* – an onomatopoeia for being slippery and slimy. The jingoemon imo is particularly nuru nuru, with a creamy, viscous consistency that melts into the stew.

Chef //
Haruki Sato
Location //
Mogami, Yamagata

IMO-NI
Taro stew

Serves 6

Preparation time: 10 mins
Cooking time: 30 mins

1kg (2 lb 3 oz) jingoemon imo (taro)
500g (1lb 2oz) block konnyaku (taro cake)
60ml (2 fl oz) dark soy sauce
30g (1 oz) sugar
1 tsp dashi powder (optional)
500g (1lb 2oz) mushrooms, trimmed
*300g (10½ oz) beef (such as rump steak, fillet or
    ribeye), thinly sliced*
2 leeks, sliced on a diagonal into 2cm (¾ in) pieces

1 Use a sharp knife to trim the taro and peel away the skin. Cut in half on a diagonal and put in a bowl of cold water while you prepare the remaining ingredients.

2 Using your hands, break off bite-sized pieces of konnyaku and put in a large saucepan. Drain the taro and add it to the pan along with enough water to cover the taro and konnyaku.

3 Set the pan over medium-high heat and stir in the soy sauce. Bring to the boil and skim off any foam that forms on the surface.

4 Add the sugar and dashi powder, if using (this gives a more flavourful broth), and cook, stirring occasionally, for about 15 minutes until the taro softens.

5 Add the mushrooms and simmer for 2–3 minutes, then add the beef. Cook for 2–3 minutes then add the leeks and cover the pan with a lid. Cook for another 2 minutes, to soften the leeks. Taste for seasoning, adding soy sauce if needed, and serve immediately.

JINGISUKAN
Smoky mutton and onions

This dish of smoky grilled mutton and onions with a garlicky sauce may seem un-Japanese to outsiders, but that's because Hokkaido is vastly different from the rest of Japan.

When Sapporoites leave home there is one food they miss more than anything –jingisukan. If you thought jingisukan sounded suspiciously like the name of a certain Mongolian conqueror, you'd be correct – though the dish is about as Mongolian as Mongolian barbecue. In the early 20th century, the government introduced sheep rearing to Hokkaido, which seemed well suited to the wide-open spaces on the island. The wool industry never did take off, but the locals developed a taste for mutton. Supermarkets in Sapporo are stocked with mutton that has been pre-marinated and ready for the grill –something you won't find in Tokyo. Nobody is exactly sure how jingisukan got its name. However, one popular theory is that the pan on which it is cooked was thought to resemble a warlord's helmet. The special pan, called a *jingisukan-nabe*, is key: its convex shape allows the juices from the mutton, which sizzle on top, to run down to the vegetables nestled around the brim. It's genius, really.

Daruma is one of Sapporo's oldest jingisukan restaurants. It opened 60 years ago in the city's nightlife district, Susukino, and still regularly draws crowds – even when the weather is below freezing. There's space for just 20 seats around the horseshoe-shaped counter, which is fitted with ten charcoal braziers. Jingisukan is a dish that diners cook themselves at the table. A chunk of mutton fat is placed on top of the pan and a handful of onions scattered below. Raw meat is ordered by the plate, along with mugs of frothy beer. The table is set with tongs; there are jars of crushed garlic and red pepper flakes to add to the sauce. 'The sauce gets better as you go, because the juices from the meat get mixed in,' says proprietress Kaneshika Sumiko. Daruma regulars know to finish the meal with a bowl of *ochayu* (rice with tea) to which the leftover sauce is added. 'It's a restorative,' says Kaneshika.

Chef //
Kaneshika Sumiko
Location //
Daurma Honten,
Sapporo, Hokkaido

JINGISUKAN
Smoky mutton and onions

Serves 4

Preparation time: 10 mins
Cooking time: 30 mins

600g (1lb 5 oz) mutton (although Daruma
   proprietress Kaneshika prefers shoulder roast,
   any cut will do)
50g (1¾ oz) mutton or beef lard, or cooking oil
2 medium onions, cut into 2.5cm (1 in) wedges
2 leeks, cut into 2.5cm (1 in) slices
320g (11½ oz) rice, cooked according to
   recipe on page 264
2.5 litres (85 fl oz) brewed Japanese green tea
   (optional)

For the sauce
150ml (5 fl oz) dark soy sauce
75ml (2½ fl oz) sake
2 cloves garlic, finely minced, or to taste
red pepper flakes or ichimi red pepper seasoning,
   to taste
1 tbsp grated ginger
2 tbsp grated apple
1 tbsp sesame seeds
1 tbsp sugar

1 First, make the dipping sauce by combining the ingredients in a small bowl. This can be done ahead of time.

2 Slice the mutton into 5mm (¼in) thick slices, removing any tendons as you do so. Score the slices in a crosshatch pattern on both sides.

3 Set a jingisukan-nabe (see below) over hot charcoal (alternatively, preheat a griddle pan or barbecue). Add half of the lard to the pan. When it starts to melt, use chopsticks or tongs to distribute the lard evenly on the surface of the pan.

4 Arrange some of the onions and leeks around the edge of the pan. When the pan is searingly hot, place a few strips of mutton in the centre, on the dome, and fry until starting to brown. Continue to cook the mutton and vegetables, in batches, adding more lard as needed, until done.

5 Divide the sauce into individual dipping bowls, adding more garlic and red pepper flakes to taste. To serve, arrange the mutton between plates and the sauce for dipping. You can serve this with cooked rice if you are not doing the next step.

6 *This step is optional:* Once the meat and vegetables have been eaten, make a big pot of green tea and divide the rice into bowls. Pour the tea over the rice and add some of the remaining dipping sauce along with any scraps stuck to the pan.

Tip

Jingisukan is typically cooked and eaten at the table altogether, with more meat and vegetables added to the grill as you go. To make the dish at the table, use an electric hotplate or try a gas-fired camper-style stove. At a pinch, simply fry in a pan on the kitchen hob and serve as a main course.

Jingisukan-nabe are available online for purchase. They are ideal for making this dish and for marinated meat, imparting a smoky barbecued aroma.

MENME YU-NI
Braised whole fish wrapped in kombu

Yu-ni means 'to boil', and in Rausu it implies boiling with a local ingredient, kombu. Here, Hiromi Ishida prepares the briny, mineral-rich seaweed with delicate thornyhead fish, menme.

Rausu is a small fishing town situated in the remote eastern Hokkaido that is defined by the sea. At night, the lights of night-fishing boats illuminate the streets along the harbour, making streetlights unnecessary. The seasons are marked by the catch: squid in the autumn; octopus in the winter; sea urchin in the spring; kelp in the summer. 'Even if they're not out on a boat, pretty much everyone here has something to do with the sea,' says Hiromi Ishida, a home cook who moved from Sapporo to Rausu when she married a local fisherman. She herself is a member of the local fishing cooperative, where her roles include cooking for festivals and for visiting school groups.

In the winter, the Arctic current brings nutrient-rich ice floes to the waters around Rausu, which locals credit for the abundant (and flavourful) marine life here. Of everything that comes out of the sea, it is the kombu, which is harvested off the coast in summer, that is most prized. Rausu kombu makes the richest stock and is a favourite among chefs working in exclusive *kaiseki* (haute cuisine) restaurants. Naturally, the locals set aside a portion of the harvest for themselves. Ishida explains that there are two ways to make yu-ni: the way you make it for your family and the way you make it for guests. 'If you're cooking for yourself at home, you can just throw in chunks of fish and a few pieces of kombu [into the pan],' she says. If serving guests, the recipe on page 54 is used where a whole fish is wrapped up in the soft, leathery kombu kelp, tied with a ribbon of *kampyo* (dried gourd) and served up like a parcel. Thornyhead, with its vibrant, auspicious colouring, is a luxury fish also caught locally. When it comes to menme yu-ni, the cooking process is almost effortless, but the rewards are high: 'All the flavour of the kombu goes into the fish,' says Ishida.

Chef //
Hiromi Ishida
Location //
Rausu, Hokkaido

MENME YU-NI

Braised whole fish wrapped in kombu

Serves 2

Preparation time: 10 mins
Cooking time: 15 mins

2 whole firm-fleshed white fish (about 400g/14 oz
   each), such as thornyhead, cleaned and scaled
2 x 30cm (12 in) sheets kombu, large enough to
   wrap around fish (or if the sheets are thin use 2
   per fish)
1 x 50g (1¾ oz) packet plain (unflavoured)
   kampyo (dried gourd) strips
2 tbsp sea salt

1 Rinse and pat the fish dry with paper towels. Wrap tightly in kombu, securing with strips of kampyo at both the ends.

2 Place the fish in a large stockpot and fill with enough water to cover the fish. Add the salt and bring to the boil over high heat. Reduce the heat to medium-low and simmer for 10–15 minutes, or until the flesh of the fish is opaque and cooked through.

3 Carefully remove the parcel-wrapped fish and serve as is to be untied at the table. Although the kombu and kampyo are edible, most of their flavour has been soaked up by the fish during the cooking process.

Tip

Ishida also prepares this dish with pollock. If you can't find either pollock or thornyhead, any mild-tasting, firm, white-fleshed fish will do.

Kampyo (dried gourd)

Strips of dried gourd, also known as kampyo, are sold in small packets at most Asian supermarkets. Though edible, kampyo is most often used for food presentation.

ZUNDA MOCHI
Crushed soybean rice cakes

The bright – almost lurid – green of fresh soybeans signals summer. In Sendai, they're used in this sweet dish, traditionally eaten as a pick-me-up during the hottest days of the year.

Soybeans are a staple of Japanese cooking – appearing in miso, *natto* (a fermented soybean) and tofu – and they grow plentifully in the fields around Tohoku's largest city, Sendai. Edamame are young soybeans, harvested in the summer, a few months earlier than the ones that then go on to become tofu. Usually edamame are boiled and eaten with salt, served still in their pods in a wicker basket next to a frothy mug of a beer. Sendai, however, has a curious way of eating them: crushed into a paste and spiked with sugar, spread over springy cakes of pounded rice (mochi). According to Hiromi Hosoya, the owner of Endo Mochiten, edamame have been enjoyed in this way longer than anyone can remember. Local legend says that the feudal warlord (and famous gourmand) who ruled Sendai in the 1600s, Date Matsumura, was a fan.

Hosoya's parents opened Endo Mochiten on an otherwise nondescript street in downtown Sendai in 1948. The shop is easy to spot; the outside is painted the same vibrant green as edamame. 'My dad thought it would be best to stand out,' says Hosoya with a laugh. The small kitchen in the back of the shop is full of curious vintage machines: one with a long arm that pounds the rice for mochi with a rhythmic thwack; another that whirrs as it grinds the beans into paste. There are giant bamboo steamer baskets full of beans and trays of mochi, dusted with *katakuriko* (vegetable starch), that look like melting marshmallows. 'We make zunda mochi like it used to be made with just edamame, sugar and a tiny bit of salt. Not too much sugar. Just enough to bring out the natural sweetness of the beans,' says Hosoya.

Zunda mochi has a fresh, verdant taste and a subtle sweetness that pairs well with green tea. Hosoya says you can reduce the amount of sugar and serve the crushed beans atop summer vegetables, such as aubergine.

Chef //
Hiromi Hosoya
Location //
Endo Mochiten, Sendai

ZUNDA MOCHI
Crushed soybean rice cakes

Serves 6

Preparation time: 30 mins plus cooling time
Cooking time: 10 mins

500g (1lb 2oz) fresh edamame, or podded
  and frozen
180g (6½ oz) sugar
pinch of salt
270g (9½ oz) mochi (Japanese glutinous rice
  cake) (see tip)

1 If using fresh edamame, pop the beans from their pods and peel off the thin layer of skin enclosing each bean.

2 Steam the podded beans for 10 minutes in a bamboo steamer or in a sieve suspended over a pan of simmering water.

3 Remove the beans from the steamer and transfer to a food processor. Add the sugar and salt and pulse briefly to form a rough paste – don't over process the beans, you're looking for some texture.

4 Spread the bean mixture evenly in a shallow tin and let it cool to room temperature.

5 Place the mochi in the pan with the beans and frost both sides of each with the bean paste. If the paste is too thick to spread, add a splash of hot water and mix before adding to the mochi.

Tip

Most Asian grocery stores will carry ready-made mochi, but these don't compare to homemade ones. Several Japanese home appliance makers sell tabletop mochi makers where all you need to do is add rice and water (available online).

SEA OF JAPAN

WAJIMA ●⑩

③

⑩

Toyama Bay

● Toyama

● Kanazawa

⑥

⑧ NAGANO ●

RIKKOMAN

Maebashi ●

⑮

UTSUNOMIYA

Mito ●

⑦

● Takayama

● Matsumoto

● Fukui

⑭

Kofu ●

TOKYO ●

● Kamakura

● Nagoya

⑨

SHIZUOKA ●

Sagami-nada Sea

Ise Bay

Suruga Bay

● Hamamatsu

PACIFIC OCEAN

Asakus

⑤

Ueno

① ●

Chiyoda-ku

Chūō-ku

⑬

Shinjuku-ku

TOKYO

④

② ● Ginza

Tsukiji

⑫

Roppongi

Shibuya-ku

Koto-ku

Meguro-ku

⑪

Minato-ku

TOKYO & CENTRAL JAPAN

Tokyo's modern cuisine, like that of many thriving capital cities, blends tradition with flavours from around the globe. To the west, Nagano and the Japan Alps are regions of hearty mountain fare

EBISHINJYO
Crisp-fried prawn balls

*Zaiyu Hasegawa
puts a playful
spin on kaiseki,
multi-course
meals, at the ultra-
refined yet relaxed
Jimbocho Den. His
signature is taking
humble dishes, like
ebishinjyo, to new
heights.*

K aiseki is a culinary tradition blending regional cooking with the ritual
traditions of imperial banquet and Buddhist temple cuisines. *Kaiseki* chefs
follow the philosophy of *shun*, using ingredients at their most flavourful and
vibrant. Ingredients are used not simply for the way they taste but also for what they
symbolise, from the seasons to prosperity and success. The result is an elaborate
procession of breathtaking plates that tell a story. Prominent French chefs visiting
Japan in the 1970s were so blown away, they returned to France with ideas for the
degustation menu, which in turn spawned the tasting menus that define today's
Western high-end cuisine.

At Den, even salad isn't simple. Zaiyu prepares each vegetable differently: one is raw,
another pickled, braised, roasted, fermented or fried. To keep things from getting too
serious, a surprise soybean or two branded with a smiley face hides among the leaves.

Zaiyu grew up in the fine-dining world, eating sushi his mother brought home
from a renowned *ryotei* (luxury restaurant) in Kagurazaka, where she performed as
a geisha. Eventually, he began cooking as an apprentice there.

This style of ebishinjyo is distinct to the Tokyo region, he says, as it traditionally
uses succulent *shiba-ebi*, a strongly flavoured prawn once fished in the Tokyo Bay.

'It is a dish I learned at the ryotei, the first dish I was permitted to serve to guests,'
Zaiyu says. He was 18 and nervous, and his leap towards innovation had not yet
begun. Even so, he says, 'I still cook this whenever I have the right ingredients
available as it reminds me of my beginnings.'

Though the recipe is simple, getting the ebishinjyo crisp and light is a matter of
mastery. Zaiyu's speciality is precisely this, transforming the humble fried prawn
ball into something of sophistication.

Chef //
Zaiyu Hasegawa
Location //
Jimbocho Den, Tokyo

EBISHINJYO
Crisp-fried prawn balls

Serves 2

Preparation time: 30 min
Cooking time: 10–15 min

200g (7 oz) prawns, shelled and deveined
½ small onion, very finely chopped
50g (1¾ oz) katakuriko (potato starch)
½ egg yolk, about 30g (1 oz)
125ml (4 fl oz) vegetable oil plus extra for
*   deep-frying*
2 generous pinches salt plus extra to serve

1 Take half the prawns and use a sharp knife to finely chop them into a smooth paste. This will take about 10 minutes of continuous chopping. Alternatively, use a food processor.

2 Chop the remaining prawns more coarsely, leaving the pieces about the size of rice grains.

3 Gently squeeze the onion in a clean cloth to remove excess moisture. Put the onion in a small bowl with about 10g (¼ oz) of the katakuriko, just enough to coat the onion evenly. Set aside.

4 In a bowl, whisk the egg yolk. Pour in the oil gradually, a drop at a time, whisking continuously, to make an emulsion. Once emulsified, continue to add the rest of the oil slightly faster, whisking continuously to form a mayonnaise-like consistency. Set aside.

5 In a large bowl, combine both types of chopped prawns, the onion and starch mixture and the egg. Shape the prawn mixture into golfball-sized balls (weighing about 40g/1½ oz each) and place on a plate.

6 Pour enough oil in a deep, wide pan to come up to about 3cm (1¼ in). Place over medium heat and bring up to 180°C/350°F (use a thermometer). The very hot oil should bubble vigorously when a chopstick is inserted.

7 Slide in the prawn balls, adding them in batches so as not to overcrowd the pan. Cook for 3–5 minutes, turning using a wooden spoon, until the balls are golden brown all over. Season with salt and serve hot.

TOMOROKOSHI TEMPURA

Corn tempura

Chef Fumio Kondo of Tempura Kondo has been credited with bringing tempura, battered morsels, to the modern day, infusing it with an airy crispness and the earthiness of seasonal vegetables.

Tempura has a special place in the hearts of Tokyoites who have been perfecting it for centuries. The idea of battering and frying is believed to have arrived on Japanese shores via Portuguese traders in the 1600s. It soon found a following in Tokyo (then the feudal capital Edo), becoming part of the city's lively and precocious dining culture. Of course Tokyo has seen many more imports over the centuries, but tempura remains vital: there is a fast-food chain that specialises in it, and also several high-end restaurants.

Tempura Kondo falls into the latter category. Chef Fumio Kondo has been making tempura for 50 years, and like most chefs who make tempura, he makes nothing else. His two Michelin star restaurant is located, alongside a good percentage of the city's top restaurants, in Tokyo's elegant, upmarket Ginza district. However, Fumio's lack of pretension aligns him less with his immediate neighbours and more with the city's historic working class quarters – where he grew up. Six days a week he rises early to visit Tokyo's central wholesale market to select the most tempting seasonal seafood and produce, around which he designs the menu for the day. He cooks both lunch and dinner at the counter across from his diners, serving just one piece at a time.

'The ingredients are so simple, just flour and eggs!' Fumio says. The trick is in the timing: every ingredient has its own optimal cooking time, and that's where practice comes in. Fumio can tell when a piece is ready from across the room just by listening to how it sings in the oil. Traditionally, tempura was made from seafood. Fumio created a minor (and much-copied) culinary revolution when he turned to vegetables. Fried with his signature light touch, they emerge plump and moist. Any vegetable with a decent heft can be made into tempura. Corn tempura is a summer speciality at Tempura Kondo and the highlight of the season's tasting menu.

Chef //
Fumio Kondo
Location //
Tempura Kondo, Tokyo

TOMOROKOSHI TEMPURA
Corn tempura

Serves 8 as a starter

Preparation time: 10 min
Cooking time: 15–20 min

sesame oil, for deep-frying
250ml (8½ fl oz) ice-cold water
½ egg, about 30g
250g (9 oz) plain flour plus
   2 tbsp extra
5 corncobs, husks removed
   and kernels cut
sea salt, for serving

1 Add enough sesame oil to a large wok or pan to come up to 3cm (1¼ in). Heat to 180°C (350°F).

2 While the oil is heating, fill a container (cylindrical shape is best) or bowl with the ice-cold water. Add the egg and whisk vigorously, making sure the egg white is thoroughly mixed. Skim off any foam that forms on the surface.

3 Pour half the egg and water mixture into a bowl and add 125g (4½ oz) flour. Whisk using a gentle folding motion, being careful not to be too brisk as this will cause the batter to become gluey. Gradually, add the remaining egg and water mixture, along with the remaining flour, and stir. The mixture should be runny, like milk rather than milkshake.

4 Mix 6 tablespoons of corn kernels with 2 tbsp flour to dredge, then transfer to the batter and coat gently.

5 If you don't have a cooking thermometer, check the oil temperature by dribbling some batter into the hot oil. When the pan is ready, the oil should spit.

6 Using a slotted spoon, scoop half the corn out of the batter and slide it gently into the oil, keeping the corn together in a mound as much as possible. Return errant kernels to the fold with metal chopsticks. Once the collection of corn becomes solid, pile on more battered corn little by little to make one giant tempura, and continue to fry until the base is golden and crispy. Flip over to cook the other side, until cooked through (the bubbles at the edges of the tempura will begin to subside).

7 Use a slotted spoon to remove the tempura and slide it, in one piece, onto paper towels to absorb excess oil. Repeat with the remaining mixture until done. Serve immediately with a dish of sea salt on the side for dipping.

Tip

Tempura is best cooked one piece at a time. Adding too many pieces at once can lower the oil temperature, which can result in the final product being too oily.

KONKA SABA TO GOHAN
Fermented mackerel with rice

Italian-trained Australian chef Ben Flatt fell in love with Noto Peninsula's tradition of fermentation two decades ago. His classic rice dish features pungent fermented fish distinctive of this region.

Noto Peninsula is a rugged strip of land, dotted with small fishing villages caught between the sea and the rocky interior. Cut off from the Japanese mainland by geography and climate much of the year, Noto developed a food culture centred on fermentation.

Traditional households in Noto still keep a stock of fermented foods in the *shokeba*, a storeroom near the kitchen reserved especially for turning yellow plums into umeboshi, soybeans into miso, and squid guts into ishiri. Here on the peninsula, ishiri was used as a seasoning even before soy sauce.

At their ryokan, Ben and his wife and partner, Chikako, make their ishiri using the methods Chikako's father Toshihiro, a celebrated fermentation master, perfected. They mix squid guts with salt, then leave it for several years, at least, until it has transformed into a dark, intensely umami seasoning.

They also use the abundant local mackerel and sardines to make konka saba and konka iwashi, fermented mackerel and sardines. The quantities of ingredients and time required depend greatly on climate and humidity. It is made by packing alternating layers of the fish with *nuka* (fermented rice bran), sliced red chillies and salt in a bucket, and leaving it for at least a year or two. The process recalls the earliest forms of sushi, fish preserved in fermented rice, introduced in the 8th century from China.

'We just finished some konka iwashi made 15 years ago,' Chikako says. 'The flavour was intense; you could say, extreme.'

In the decades Ben has been in Japan, he has learned to seamlessly fuse his understanding of Italian cuisine, working with the ingredients he has on hand. At the ryokan, he serves konka saba in an Italian olive oil and garlic sauce over pasta for dinner, then in the morning he serves it again with rice (see recipe) as part of a traditional Japanese breakfast.

'These fermentation methods are slowly disappearing,' Ben says. 'We feel it's our responsibility to keep them alive by using them in new and old, delicious ways.'

Chef //
Ben Flatt
Location //
Chikako Funashita,
Ishikawa Prefecture

KONKA SABA TO GOHAN
Fermented mackerel with rice

Serves 2

Preparation time: 20 mins
Cooking time: 10 mins

220g (8 oz) cooked short-grain rice (see page 264)
1 konka saba (fermented mackerel) fillet, cut into 1cm (½ in) steaks, or 2 large anchovy fillets, drained
1 kaki no ha (persimmon leaf), or aluminium foil

1 Preheat the irori (charcoal grill) until the charcoal is bright red.

2 Place the konka saba on the *kaki no ha* (or a piece of foil), on the edge of the grill (not on the hottest spot) and cook until the fish starts to release its juices, about 6–7 minutes. Turn over and grill for another few minutes until the fish is heated through.

3 Divide the cooked rice between serving bowls and arrange the fish on top. It pairs well with a bright *jyunmai* sake – 'but perhaps not for breakfast,' says Ben.

> ## *Tip*
>
> *Fermented rice bran is also used in other parts of Japan for turning aubergine, daikon, cucumber, and cabbage into pickles called nukazuke. When used for pickling, the bran is sometimes roasted, then fermented in a mash with water and salt.*

IWASHI SUSHI
Sardine sushi

Sushi, Japan's most iconic dish, is simply raw fish and vinegar-seasoned rice. Ryuichi Yui specialises in the traditional Tokyo style.

That sushi should be as fresh as possible is actually misleading. 'Sometimes I'll buy fish and think, "this will be tastier tomorrow",' says Ryuichi Yui of Kizushi. At 73, the third-generation chef still takes his moped to the fish market every morning to shop for ingredients.

Sushi was traditionally used as a way to preserve fish – that's the reason for the vinegar in the rice. It only got fresher, and faster to make, once modern transportation and refrigeration entered the picture. Older shops like Kizushi straddle the line between the traditional and the modern. Ryuichi's style of sushi, called *edo-mae* after the old name for Tokyo, Edo, emerged around the turn of the last century. This is *nigiri-zushi* – the hand-moulded pedestals of fish and rice that has become globally synonymous with sushi today. However, Ryuichi still uses old-fashioned preservation techniques, like salting the fish or marinating it in vinegar, methods that hark back to the days when his grandfather first opened the shop. Back then, sushi consisted only of what could be fished from Tokyo Bay, and such classic *neta* (sushi toppings) like squid, octopus, gizzard shad and conger eel are still staples at Kizushi. *Iwashi* (sardine) sushi is another example of this traditional style, and one that brings into focus the rich complexity that it can have: the oily, just slightly funky fish is dressed in salt, tart vinegar, spicy ginger and crisp spring onions.

One sushi myth that needs busting is that learning to make sushi takes years. Learning the ins and outs of running a sushi shop takes years, Ryuichi explains, but learning to make sushi, he claims, can be done in a week. During the years he spent apprenticing in his family's shop – making tea and going on delivery runs – he practised his rice moulding technique with *okara* (soy pulp) because rice, of course, was too precious to waste.

Chef //
Ryuichi Yui
Location //
Kizushi, Tokyo

IWASHI SUSHI
Sardine sushi

Serves 2 (makes 12 pieces of sushi)

Preparation time: 35 min

For the sardines

12 sardines, filleted
150ml (5 fl oz) white vinegar
150ml (5 fl oz) red vinegar (preferably made
from sake lees, if available)
1 tbsp finely grated ginger
1 tbsp finely chopped spring onion (scallion)
200ml (7 fl oz) water
soy sauce, for brushing
salt

For the sushi rice

100g short-grain rice, cooked according
to the recipe on page 264
½ tbsp white vinegar
½ tbsp red vinegar (preferably made from
sake lees, if available)
¾ tsp salt

Tip

There are a few different classic styles
of hand-moulding for nigiri-sushi.
Ryuichi practises what he calls the
'waltz' school, a 1–2–3 passing of the
sushi between both hands three times.

---

1 Place the sardine fillets, skin-side down, and salt generously. Leave to sit for 15 minutes.

2 In the meantime, mix the two vinegars for the sardines in a measuring jug (cup). Pour 200ml (7 fl oz) of the mixture into a shallow bowl. Pour the remaining mixture into a separate shallow dish along with 200ml (7 fl oz) water – this will be the mixture for dipping your hands.

3 Place the cooked rice in a large bowl and add both vinegars and the salt. Use a spatula to turn the rice, allowing it to cool until almost at room temperature.

4 Rinse the sardine fillets thoroughly under cold running water to remove the salt. Slice the fillets in half lengthways and quickly immerse in the vinegar mixture. Then pat dry with paper towels and gently peel off the skin, using your hands.

5 Dip your hands into the water and vinegar mixture – this prevents sticking. Take a small amount of sushi rice, about 1 tablespoon, in one hand. Using a few quick motions shape into an oblong being careful not to squeeze too firmly, but firm enough for it to keep its shape.

6 Using your other hand, hold two pieces of fish, overlapping so that the fish will overhang the rice, skin-side down, in the palm of your hand. Put a dollop of ginger and a sprinkling of chives on the underside of the fish, and then place the rice on the fish. With a back and forth motion, three times, use both hands to gently press the fish and rice together.

7 Brush the top with soy sauce and place on a serving dish. Continue making the sushi until done, wetting your hands as necessary. Serve immediately.

GYU SHIGURE ONIGIRI

Rice balls stuffed with sweet soy beef

Onigiri, rice balls filled with tasty morsels, are Japan's answer to the sandwich – portable and infinitely customisable. For Yosuke Miura's grandmother, an onigiri master, the secret was perfect rice.

Yadoroku is the oldest onigiri shop in Tokyo. '*Yado* means "home", and *roku* comes from *rokudenashi*, the word for "lazy bum",' Yosuke says. 'My grandmother always said she had to open this shop because of the *rokudenashi* – my grandfather.'

When Yadoroku served its first onigiri in 1954, white rice was still a luxury. Today, onigiri are in every *conbini* (convenience store) across Japan. Miura distinguishes his onigiri by still treating rice as precious, even wrapping takeaway orders in *kyougi* (thin sheets of spruce) instead of plastic.

At Yadoroku, onigiri are served warm, compressed just enough for each grain of rice to melt away with each bite, and the *nori* (seaweed) they are customarily wrapped in, still crisp. Yosuke offers more than 20 kinds of fillings at a time, with a few daily specials. On the menu might be onigiri filled with *umeboshi* (pickled plum), salted salmon, *shirasu* (baby anchovies), ginger in miso paste, *yamagobo* (mountain burdock), or a selection of lightly pickled vegetables.

In Tokyo today, onigiri are most commonly shaped into triangles, representing harmony with nature in the Shinto tradition. In other parts of Japan, they may be ovals, gumdrops, or spheres. Lucky children find Hello-Kitty-shaped onigiri in their lunchboxes.

To get the rice right, Yosuke generally uses Koshihikari rice, a fragrant short-grain variety from the Niigata Prefecture. 'If the qualities of the harvest change, I use other varieties to make sure I achieve just the right stickiness and flavour,' Yosuke says. For his fillings, he picks up ideas wandering around Tsukiji Market and on his travels. He is also inspired by recipes on the internet: 'Even with tradition you have to keep things fresh.'

Chef //
Yosuke Miura
Location //
Onigiri Asakusa
Yadoroku, Tokyo

GYU SHIGURE ONIGIRI

Rice balls stuffed with sweet soy beef

Serves 1-2 (makes 4 rice balls)

Preparation time: 30 minutes
Cooking time: 1½ hours

2–4 sheets nori (depending on size)
4 takuan (pickled daikon) slices
salt, for sprinkling

For the beef

200g (7 oz) beef, very thinly sliced, ask
   your butcher to slice sirloin for you
1 tbsp water
3 tbsp sake
2 tbsp mirin
3 tbsp dark soy sauce
3mm (⅛ in) slice ginger
pinch of dried ground sansho
   (Japanese pepper)
1 tbsp sugar

For the rice

150g (5½ oz) short-grain rice
180ml (6 fl oz) water

Tip

*Try to have both rice and
filling hot and ready to serve
at the same time. For a
vegetarian version, the beef
can easily be substituted for
vegetables such as shiitake
mushrooms or root vegetables.*

---

1 First, sauté the beef in a pan over medium-low heat until the meat starts to colour. (There is no need to use cooking oil if your beef is sufficiently fatty.) Add the water, and then the sake, mirin, soy sauce, and gently simmer for a few minutes. As the liquid begins to cook off, add the ginger, sansho and sugar, then partially cover with a lid. Simmer, keeping an eye on the heat and being careful not to let it scorch, for another few minutes, or until most of the liquid has evaporated.

2 Rinse the rice under cold running water until it runs clear. (Miura prefers to leave some bran, so he only washes a few times.) Leave the rice to drain for 30 minutes in a strainer.

3 Combine the rice and water in a large saucepan, cover with a lid with a heavy weight on top and leave for 1 hour. Then set over high heat. When it comes to the boil, reduce the heat to medium-low and cook for a further 18 minutes, until the steam subsides and the rice is just tender.

4 Turn off the flame, then leave the rice to rest with the lid still on for 15 minutes. Loosen the rice with a paddle when you are ready to shape it.

5 *To shape the onigiri*: While the rice is still warm – but not hot or cold, otherwise it won't stick together properly – lightly moisten very clean hands with water, then sprinkle a little salt on one palm. Pat your hands together to distribute the salt and dust off any excess. Take a handful of rice (about 70g/2½ oz) in one hand and, using the other hand to apply very light pressure, shape it into a flat circle and make an indentation in the centre.

6 Put a scant teaspoon of the filling into the hole then gently mould and press the rice over the filling to seal. Continue to turn and press the rice to form a triangle.

7 Cut a strip of nori at least twice as long and a little wider than the base of the rice triangle. Wrap a nori strip around each rice ball, leaving one end of the nori a few inches unstuck at the back. Serve immediately with the takuan.

Yosuke still uses his grandmother's original wooden mould to shape his onigiri. The edges are now so worn, he jokes, customers get a better deal with larger portions every day. Shaping rice in a mould without overdoing it is a test of mastery. For beginners, start with your hands and a flat surface.

YASEI KINOKO: NAMEKO SHABUSHABU TO SHIITAKE NO SUMIBIYAKI

Wild mushrooms: Nameko hotpot and grilled shiitake

In Nagano's snow-capped mountains, Akihiko Kadowaki forages for wild mushrooms among the pine needles every autumn. He prepares them simply. He cooks accompaniments in the hot springs his village has relied on for hundreds of years.

Akihiko and his wife Setsuko run Marunaka Lodge, a small *minshuku* (guesthouse) in the village of Nozawa, nestled below Mount Kenashi. It is on these slopes that he forages for wild mushrooms in the autumn.

Nagano, with its cool, humid inland climate, is famed for its fungi. Today nearly all mushrooms cultivated in Japan originate here with 5 per cent grown in the wild. Only a handful of people still forage for them like Akihiko.

He learned how to forage in part by following the nose of the *kamoshika* (a Japanese serow that looks like a cross between mountain goat and wild boar). 'They always know which are the most flavourful,' Akihiko says. He later took up *genbokusaibai*, a method of wild cultivation where logs of oak and beechwood on the forest floor are inoculated with tiny spores.

Though wild and supermarket mushrooms may look the same, the difference between their flavours and textures are stark. Wild *nameko*, an amber-hued, gelatinous mushroom, is boldly earthy and pleasantly chewy, while genbokusaibai shiitake has an intense umami taste with a texture not too different from tender steak.

During autumn, Akihiko will take guests out to forage for mushrooms. Many of the mushrooms served at the guesthouse can only be foraged in the Nagano mountains, which is a good enough reason to visit Nozawa.

Another is to experience the natural hot springs that bubble up here. At the centre of the village, three springs flow into open pools that have been reserved for cooking since 1557. Each spring holds a steady temperature of 90°C, 80°C and 70°C respectively, and Akihiko uses them for blanching vegetables. He says, when living off what the land provides, he likes to keep things simple.

Chef //
Akihiko Kadowaki
Location //
Marunaka Lodge, Nagano

YASEI KINOKO: NAMEKO SHABUSHABU TO SHIITAKE NO SUMIBIYAKI

Wild mushrooms: Nameko hotpot and grilled shiitake

Serves 2

Preparation time: 1 hr
Cooking time: 30 mins

2 nameko mushrooms (ideally, wild ones that have grown to about 10cm/4 in diameter, or if such large ones aren't available, use bunches of small nameko)
1 lemon
fine sea salt or dark soy sauce, for seasoning
1 shiitake mushroom

1 Prepare the nameko mushrooms by trimming off any woody parts from the stems. Soak the mushrooms in a bowl of water for 1 hour.

2 Meanwhile for the shiitake, preheat a shichirin (a small, tabletop grill) until the charcoal is bright red. Alternatively, preheat your grill (broiler) to high. Prepare the shiitake by wiping with a clean dry cloth. Trim off any woody parts from the stems, keeping the stems as much as possible.

3 When you are ready to cook, sprinkle the underside of the shiitake with a little salt. Grill the shiitake for 2–3 minutes, or until they are lightly charred and have started to sweat a little.

4 Meanwhile, bring a saucepan of water to the boil and blanch the nameko for 1–2 minutes. When tiny bubbles escape from the mushrooms, they are ready. Remove and drain. Squeeze lemon on the underside of the mushroom caps and sprinkle with a little salt, or soy sauce.

5 Serve the shiitake stem side up, and eat with your hands. Serve the nameko hot, with chopsticks.

Ingredients that speak

In Japanese cooking, ingredients are chosen for reasons beyond just flavour. Colours and shapes can symbolise good omens, while names are often puns for a deeper message. These meanings derive from Buddhist and Chinese customs and come into play mostly during holidays when special meals are served. During Hinamatsuri, the annual spring festival for women and girls, the colour of foods mean a lot. Mochi, pounded rice cakes, come in all shades: white (fertility), pink (purity), green (longevity) or yellow (spring and new beginnings). For New Year celebrations, families eat kuromame, plump black soybeans, to bring success ('mame' is a pun for diligence), and datemaki, rolled egg omelettes, for wisdom, as the shape resembles a scroll.

HOBAMISO
Miso on a magnolia leaf

Nobuko Kitahira keeps her venerable ryokan's traditions alive. It was here that her grandmother-in-law began serving hobamiso, a miso simmered on the giant leaves of the white bark magnolia.

H obamiso is a Gifu speciality, which like many regional dishes, arose from humble necessity. During winters, the people of Gifu were left with few options for food except for what was preserved. At the centre of every household stood an *irori*, an open fire pit used for heating and cooking. As well as hanging pots over the fire, families used large stones encircling the irori like hot plates. Potatoes or *nimono* (simmered vegetables) were cooked or reheated directly on these stones, with a dollop of miso simmering alongside for dipping.

In 1954, Nobuko Kitahira's enterprising predecessor Haruko Kitahira put a spin on this local practice. Instead of cooking foods directly on the stone, she served the warmed miso on the beautiful leaves of the *hoba* (magnolia), which impart a fragrant, earthy aroma, and were, until then, most commonly used like today's cling film to save foods for later. Hobamiso soon became a mainstay on Gifu menus.

The ryokan, Busuitei, has stood overlooking the confluence of two rivers since the 19th century. It withstood numerous fires and typhoons until a decade ago, a devastating flood forced the family to rebuild. A centuries-old house was moved from nearby to restore the original structure.

Today Nobuko's husband Tsuguji does the cooking, while Nobuko runs the house. Many ryokans operate with three generations working side-by-side, with traditions passed from the *oo-okami* (grand hostess) to *okami* and *waka-okami* (junior hostess).

'When I got married and moved into this house, the third generation was already quite elderly, and I knew I would have to learn everything right away,' Nobuko says. 'My mother-in-law taught me how to make hobamiso. It must always be served with rice. Even though tastes have changed and some people try to avoid eating as much rice these days, the saying is that good hobamiso makes you *enjoy* your rice.'

Chef //
Nobuko & Tsuguji Kitahira
Location //
Busuitei, Mukaimachi

HOBAMISO

Miso on a magnolia leaf

Serves 2-4

Preparation time: 15 mins
Cooking time: 10 mins

100g (3½ oz) shinshu (light brown) miso
35g (1¼ oz) sugar
8g (¼ oz) mature ginger, coarsely grated and
* then drained of liquid by squeezing through*
* muslin (cheesecloth)*
1 tbsp vegetable oil
80g (2¾ oz) spring onions (scallions),
* thinly sliced*
2 hoba leaves (newly fallen leaves that are
* at least 25cm/10 in in length), or*
* parchment paper*
cooked rice, to serve

1. Prepare a shichirin (a small tabletop grill) and get the charcoal red hot. If you don't have a shichirin or hoba leaves, you can also make this dish on the stove in a roasting tin lined with parchment paper.

2. In a bowl, combine the miso, sugar, ginger, and vegetable oil to form a paste. Stir in the spring onions.

3. Rinse the hoba leaves in water and drain, but don't wipe them dry. Place the leaves on the grill, over the very hot charcoal, and spread the miso mixture over the centre of the leaf, making sure not to cover more than about a third of the leaf's surface.

4. Allow to simmer for 2 minutes, cooking until the spring onion becomes tender and the miso caramelised. When it is ready, the leaf will release a slightly smoky, autumnal aroma.

5. Serve with a bowl of rice. Nobuko says this also goes very well with a crisp sake.

OYAKI
Vegetable buns

At her snack shop, near Nagano's Zenko Temple, Tomoe Yoshikawa and the ladies, known as the 'Farmers' Mothers', entice passersby with oyaki, a crisp and chewy bun stuffed with vegetables.

Chef //
Tomoe Yoshikawa
Location //
Sanyasou, Nagano

Tomoe opened Sanyasou over a decade ago as part of an effort to get local produce back on the menus in Nagano. As the mountainous region developed into a destination for vacationing urbanites, farmers were getting pushed out. As her own shop grew, Tomoe brought in others like herself. 'Many of us have children who are farmers, so often one of us needs to leave to help harvest the apples or the grapes,' she says. 'We all understand and swap shifts to help each other out.'

It was another farmers' mother, an oyaki master in a nearby town, who taught the ladies how to make the regional snack. They are buns made from a chewy, unleavened dough, filled with pickles or soy-simmered vegetables, then cooked on the edge of the *irori*, the open fire pit at the heart of traditional Japanese homes. Oyaki vary by village in Nagano – some might use wheat, buckwheat, rice, or even rice wrapped in oak leaves instead of the dough.

At Sanyasou, the oyaki are made from wheat flour, steamed, and then finished in a pan until lightly golden. The fillings include whatever the Nagano farmers are growing – *kabocha* (a sweet squash), *azuki* (red beans), and *nozawana* (salted, leafy turnip greens) are winter staples. In spring the buds of the bitter *fukinoto* (butterbur sprout), in summer, sweet onion or slices of spicy myoga (a ginger variety), and in autumn, daikon leaves are popular.

When housing developments took over, Tomoe and her husband sold their own rice and apple farm, which had been 10 minutes from the restaurant. 'Sadly, there are no farms right nearby any more. Our friends grow their produce at the foot of the mountains, an hour away by car,' she says. Tomoe managed to keep a small plot for a garden, enough still to feed her family.

'So actually, we aren't only farmers' mothers,' she says. 'We are farmers, too.'

OYAKI
Vegetable bun

Serves 4–6 (makes about 20 buns)

Preparation time: 2½ hrs
Cooking time: 15 mins

For the dough
300g (10½ oz) wholemeal flour
50g (1¾ oz) cake/self-raising flour
250ml (8½ fl oz) water

For the filling
2kg (4 lb 6 oz) mixed shredded cabbage,
* finely cut daikon (white radish) and*
* carrot*
160g (5½ oz) yellow miso
40g (1½ oz) sugar
4 tbsp vegetable oil
1 tbsp basic dashi (see page 265)
* or water*

Vegetable and sweet miso
1 aubergine or daikon, finely sliced

For the sweet miso sauce
300g (10½ oz) yellow miso
100g (3½ oz) sugar
50ml (1½ fl oz) vegetable oil
1 tbsp basic dashi (see page 265)
* or water*

Sweet potato with sweet red
* bean paste*
2 sweet potatoes, peeled and thinly
* sliced into rounds*
225g (8 oz) red bean paste, sweetened
* to taste*
salt, for seasoning

1 Working the dough correctly is key. Combine the two flours in a large bowl and then add the water slowly, mixing with chopsticks, just until combined. Cover with cling film and allow the dough to stand for 2 hours.

2 Meanwhile, prepare the filling. Steam the vegetables in a steamer until just tender but still retaining a bit of bite. Remove, allow to cool, then squeeze out excess liquid. Put the steamed vegetables in a large bowl.

3 In a bowl, combine the miso, sugar, vegetable oil and dashi. Pour the mixture into the bowl with the steamed vegetables and mix well.

4 Divide the vegetable filling into 20 portions and form into balls. Do the same with the dough.

5 To make the buns, take one ball of dough and place on a lightly floured surface. Use the palm of one hand to flatten (or use a rolling pin) into a small circle about 10cm (4 in) in diameter and about 2mm (¹⁄₁₂ in) thick. Try to make the centre of the dough slightly thicker than the edges.

6 Place a ball of filling in the centre. Fold over the dough and shape into a ball, pressing the edges firmly to seal.

7 Steam the oyaki in a metal steamer lined with a damp cloth for 13 minutes, until the dough looks opaque and the centre is cooked through.

8 Once steamed, serve at once. Alternatively you can fry them in a non-stick pan over medium heat for 1–2 minutes, or until each side is lightly golden.

For the vegetable and sweet miso

1 Bring a saucepan of water to the boil and blanch the aubergine for a few minutes, until softened. Remove and drain.

2 To make the sweet miso sauce, combine the miso, sugar, vegetable oil, and dashi in a bowl. Spread the miso sauce between two slices of the thinly sliced vegetables like a miso sandwich.

For the sweet potato with sweet red bean paste

1 Season the sweet potatoes with salt.

2 Spread red bean paste between two slices of sweet potato, like a miso sandwich.

SHIZUOKA CHIRASHI
Scattered seasoned rice

In Shizuoka, chirashi is a point of pride. Yumi Chiba, one of the few pre-eminent female sushi chefs in Japan, makes a version with cured fish on rice seasoned with kombu, green tea and sesame.

U ntil recently, the sushi counter has been a man's world. Some reasons offered by the incumbents have to do with women's hands being considered too warm and their palates variable. So for many years, it did not occur to Yumi to train at her family's restaurant. But after college and a series of twists and turns, like her father and uncle before her, Yumi found her place in the family business, where she discovered she has both a sensitive palate and deft touch.

Her training began 16 years ago with a stray horse mackerel that ended up in the regular fish order. She progressed to maki and then nigiri. She found the challenge of classic, Edo-mae sushi, using cured fish and specialised knife skills to shape the fish, particularly intriguing.

During the Edo period (1603–1868), sushi was made with soy- or vinegar-cured fish atop vinegared rice, all pressed together in a wooden box, and then cut into blocks or cylinders to serve. A Shizuoka teahouse at the time was famed for a dish using tuna, local sakura prawns, pickles, green tea and wasabi, known as *gomoku-zushi* (scattered sushi), the predecessor to chirashi. Yumi's chirashi is not pressed but features cured ingredients scattered, ever so carefully, over rice.

Yumi points out that women have always made sushi, albeit in the background. Her mother prepares maki in the kitchen at the restaurant, while her father, the head chef, prepares sushi at the counter.

The path to *shokunin* (master) in sushi kitchens is very strict, Yumi says. 'Many struggle to accept women, because they don't want to break the rules. But it's important that those who learn these skills be allowed to continue. There are very few families left to preserve Edo-mae sushi. If there were no female sushi chefs before, then how do you know we cannot do it?'

Chef //
Yumi Chiba
Location //
Anago Uotake Sushi,
Shizuoka

SHIZUOKA CHIRASHI

Scattered seasoned rice

Serves 4

Preparation time: 2 hrs
Cooking time: 1½ hrs

For the omelette
4 large eggs
50ml (1¾ fl oz) basic dashi (see page 265)
½ tsp light soy sauce
50g (1¾ oz) sugar
¼ tsp salt
2–3 tsp vegetable oil

For the seasoned rice
450g (1 lb) short-grain rice
few pieces dried kombu, about
  7.5cm/3 in each, rinsed
75g (2¾ oz) rice wine vinegar
60g (2 oz) sugar
20g (¾ oz) salt

For the tuna
4 tsp light soy sauce
4 tsp mirin
1 tsp sugar
4 tsp sake
2 tbsp basic dashi (see page 265)
60g (2 oz) tuna, sliced into 1½ cm
  (½ in) cubes

1 First, make the omelette. In a bowl, whisk the eggs with the dashi, soy sauce, sugar and salt.

2 Heat the oil in a tamago-yakiki (a rectangular pan for making Japanese omelettes), or non-stick frying pan, over medium-high heat. When hot, add a ladleful of the egg mixture to the pan, just enough to make a thin, even layer. Wait a few seconds for the egg to begin to set, then use a pair of chopsticks to roll the omelette into a log towards the other end of the pan. Add a bit more oil, then add another ladleful of the egg mixture, tilting the pan to coat. Wait a few seconds and then roll the log back to the other end of the pan, gathering the new layer of egg as you go. Repeat until done.

3 Remove the omelette from the pan and put on a chopping board. Trim the ends off and then slice into thin ribbons. Set aside.

4 Next, make the rice. Rinse the rice until the water runs clear and drain for 20–30 minutes in a strainer. Put the rice into a large saucepan with a lid and pour in enough water to cover by about 1cm (½ in). Add a few strips of the kombu, making sure to cover most of the surface of the rice, and cook according to the instructions on page 264.

5 Combine the vinegar, sugar and salt in a bowl, and set aside.

6 When the rice is done, remove the kombu. While the rice is still hot, sprinkle with the vinegar mixture, alternately mixing and fluffing with a paddle or large spoon.

pinch of powdered green tea (such
  as matcha)
1½ tbsp white sesame seeds, ground
pinch of katsuobushi (dried bonito
  flakes), ground
80g (2¾ oz) unagi (freshwater eel),
  precooked and sliced (available at
  Japanese markets)
20g (¾ oz) seasoned seaweed (available
  at Japanese supermarkets)
60g (2 oz) pickled mackerel, sliced
  (aji or saba will do, available at
  Japanese markets)
40g (1½ oz) squid, cleaned and cut into
  1cm (½ in) cubes
pickled ginger
grated fresh or wasabi paste
4 cherry tomatoes, quartered
1½ tbsp tobiko (flying fish roe), or
  ikura (salmon roe) (both available
  at Japanese markets)
20g (¾ oz) cooked sweet prawns,
  roughly chopped

7 To prepare the tuna, combine the soy sauce, mirin, sugar, sake and dashi in a small saucepan and bring to a boil. Remove from the heat and allow to cool completely.

8 Place the tuna cubes in a shallow bowl and pour over the now-cooled soy-mirin mixture. Allow to marinate for 5–10 minutes, until the tuna begins to darken, then remove.

9 To serve, place the rice in a wide bowl. Sprinkle with the powdered green tea, ground sesame seeds and katsuobushi. Next, arrange the seafood on top, starting with the tuna, followed by the eel, tsukudani, mackerel, squid and omelette strips, in a concentric circle, leaving space in the centre. Arrange the pickled ginger and wasabi, encircled by the tomatoes, in the centre. Lastly, scatter over the tobiko and chopped prawns.

*'If there were no female sushi
chefs ever before, then how do
you know we cannot do it?'*

BURI DAIKON TO MOZUKU NO MISO AE

Simmered yellowtail and radish, and mozuko seaweed with miso

In Wajima, life is the sea. Kouichi Tanaka works with the ama, women divers who brave the frigid waters, to source the fish and seaweed he serves at his family's inn.

Kouichi's *minshuku*, the inn he inherited from his father, stands on the near northern extreme of the Noto Peninsula, a sliver of rocky cliffs jutting out over the sea. Schools of *buri* (yellowtail) swim past here during the autumn migration. This also happens to be when the fish are at their peak in terms of flavour. Tanaka prepares the oily fish simmered with *daikon* (white radish), which as the weather cools has a lovely sweetness.

'Every home in Wajimi makes daikon buri with its own very distinctive flavour,' Kouichi says. 'When you eat this dish, you think of your mother.'

It is often the amas' husbands who are out on the boats fishing for buri, Kouichi says. They bring their catch back to land for their wives to sell. Many fishwives are actually ama in their off-season.

The first ama arrived in Wajima in the mid-16th century upon the invitation of a lord looking to profit from the rich fishing grounds. Men shirked the dangers of diving in the cold, turbulent waters, while the uncomplaining ama dove into the depths, holding their breath for minutes at a time, wearing just a *saiji* (loincloth) and *tenugui* (head wrap). By the 1960s, many ama updated their outfits with goggles and wetsuits when diving for abalone, crab, seaweed and pearls.

Today, the 150 or so active ama in Wajima are on average in their sixties, and because of decreasing populations of catch, permitted to dive only from July to September from 7am to 10am.

During their short season, they still dive for *mozuku*, a seaweed that favours warm currents five metres below. Kouichi serves it fresh with a touch of vinegar in summer, and seasoned with miso the rest of the year. The seaweed boasts a particular flavour, which is bright and briny, like a bite of the sea.

Kouichi believes so long as there is water, the ama will not disappear. Recently in Wajima, he says, seven new ama have begun training, diving alongside both their mothers and grandmothers into the sea.

Chef //
Kouichi Tanaka
Location //
Oyado Tanaka, Ishikawa
Prefecture

BURI DAIKON TO MOZUKU NO MISO AE

*Simmered yellowtail and radish,
and mozuko seaweed with miso*

Serves 4

Preparation time: 30 mins plus cooling
Cooking time: 3½ hrs

*1 daikon (white radish), top half only, peeled and cut
into 2cm (¾ in) pieces*
small handful of uncooked rice
*4 buri (yellowtail) fillets, about 220g (8 oz), ideally
cut from the back, not the belly*
3 litres basic dashi (see page 265)
250ml (8½ fl oz) sake
100ml (3½ fl oz) light soy sauce
500ml (17 fl oz) dark soy sauce
250ml (8½ fl oz) mirin
3–5 tbsp sugar
*2 thumb-sized pieces ginger, one piece cut into
thin matchsticks*

For the mozuku seaweed with miso

5 tbsp miso, made with rice koji if available
*3 spring onions (scallions), green parts only,
roughly chopped*
3 tbsp sugar
50ml (1¾ fl oz) sake
*200g (7 oz) mozuku (preferably fresh but
alternatively soak dried mozuku in water for a few
hours to soften), or shio-mozuku (salted mozuku),
rinsed well*
distilled white vinegar, to taste

Tip

*Buri, mature yellowtail that is at least
three years old, is caught during winter
and is known as kan-buri. Known for being
oily and rich, it is perfect in warming
soups on cold days. Tender and sweet
tasting young buri is called hamachi and
is generally reserved for sushi.*

1 Trim the daikon pieces using the mentori method, meaning to bevel the edges of each piece – this will stop them falling apart during cooking.

2 Place the daikon in a large saucepan with enough water to cover it, and add the rice (this will help soften the daikon). Bring to the boil over medium heat and cook for about 10 minutes. Use a slotted spoon to remove the daikon (set aside) and strain the cooking liquid in a colander set over a bowl. Return the strained liquid to the pan.

3 Preheat the irori (charcoal grill), getting the charcoal hot (alternatively, use a chargrill pan or the barbecue). Grill the buri fillets over a low flame for 5–6 minutes, flipping once, until each side begins to brown. Remove and rinse the fillets, on both sides, under freshly boiled water from the kettle – this will rinse off any oils released during cooking.

4 Place the buri, dashi, sake, soy sauces, mirin, sugar and one whole knob of ginger into the pan with the daikon cooking liquid along with the reserved cooked daikon. Simmer gently for about 1½ hours. Turn off the heat and leave to rest, covered, for 2 hours.

5 To make the mozuku seaweed, combine the miso, spring onions, sugar and sake in a bowl and set aside.

6 Rinse the mozuku under cold running water and drain. Bring a pan of water to the boil and add the mozuku. Bring the water back up to the boil and immediately remove the seaweed. Rinse well under cold running water, then allow to drain well.

7 Cut the mozuku into rough 3cm (1 in) pieces and add to the sweet miso mixture, mixing well to coat. Add the vinegar, to taste.

8 When you are ready to serve, bring the buri and daikon back to a gentle boil to heat through. Serve a few pieces of buri and daikon with some of the broth and garnish with the thinly sliced matchsticks of ginger. Enjoy with rice or on its own, and serve the mozuku on the side.

TONKATSU

Deep-fried
breaded pork cutlet

*At this Tokyo
institution
dedicated to
tonkatsu, fried
pork cutlets, Izuhi
Yoshihara masters
the secrets of
mouthwateringly
crispy crust and
impossibly
tender, succulent
pork under the
tutelage of his
father and uncles.*

onkatsu is big city food, the sort of satisfying decadence that exhausted salarymen give in to at the end of a long day, washing it all down with a cold Kirin or sake, whatever their cholesterol count.

Izuhi's grandfather Isao opened Tonki in 1939 to feed the Tokyo masses with a single, plain counter surrounding three sides of spotless but no-frills kitchen built for one purpose – to perfectly bread and fry pork.

Not much has changed with the space or the recipes over the years. Izuhi performs a delicate dance using just a thin metal skewer, moving the pork cutlet between bowls of flour and egg, and then back to the start again twice more before an even layer of breadcrumbs is gently patted on. Repeating the flour and egg steps ensures a thick, crispy crust, and is the first secret to Tonki tonkatsu, Izuhi says.

The second secret should come as no surprise. It's pork lard. After breading, each cutlet is carefully eased into a vat of bubbling lard that contains the goodness of all the lard that came before it. New lard is added to the old, Izuhi says, because the tonkatsu comes out more succulent and golden the longer it is cooked.

After the cutlet luxuriates in the flavour of tonkatsus past, it re-emerges, darkly golden and crispy on the outside, dense and juicy on the inside, the porkiest pork imaginable. Tonki offers two cuts – *rosu* (fatty) and *hire* (lean). Both are excellent, but most people find nirvana with rosu.

For balance, tonkatsu is served with fresh vegetables – a bed of shredded cabbage, a slice of tomato and a sprig of parsley or two. Tonki also includes a side of their secret tangy tonkatsu sauce and a dab of spicy mustard for good measure.

'Our method of cooking keeps the oiliness of the tonkatsu minimal,' Izuhi says. 'I think this is why older people, women, children, all appreciate it as much as the salarymen.'

Chef //
Izuhi Yoshihara
Location //
Tonki, Tokyo

TONKATSU
Deep-fried breaded pork cutlet

Serves 4

Preparation time: 10 mins
Cooking time: 20 mins

300g (10½ oz) strong bread flour
300g (10½ oz) plain flour
1 egg
4 x pork loins, about 2cm (¾ in) thick and weighing
*   160–170g (5½–6 oz)*
150g (5½ oz) white breadcrumbs, or Panko
*   breadcrumbs*
1.35kg (3 lb) pork lard or 1 litre vegetable oil, for
*   deep-frying*
salt and pepper

To serve
¼ small cabbage, shredded finely avoiding the
*   tough stems and core*
½ tomato, sliced
parsley sprig
cooked rice
tonkatsu or chuno sauce (available from
*   Japanese markets)*
spicy mustard, such as karashi (Japanese mustard)
soy sauce
mayonnaise

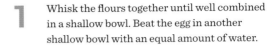

1 Whisk the flours together until well combined in a shallow bowl. Beat the egg in another shallow bowl with an equal amount of water.

2 Season the pork generously with salt and pepper. Dredge in the flour, shake off the excess, then dip into the beaten egg, allowing the excess to drip off. Repeat two more times, finishing with the egg, then use a paddle or large spoon to coat and smooth the breadcrumbs evenly all over, leaving no gaps or clumps.

3 Pour enough vegetable oil in a large pan to come up to 3cm (1¼ in). Heat the oil over medium heat to 160°C/320°F (use a thermometer). (Alternatively, if a cube of bread dropped into the hot oil sizzles for 30 seconds, the oil is ready.)

4 Carefully slide the pork into the oil, trying not to disturb the surface of the oil. The pork will sink to the bottom of the pan and soon release a steady stream of very fine bubbles. (If the bubbles are large, reduce the heat slightly.) When the pork rises to the surface, gently flip it and fry the other side; it should take about 18–20 minutes in total. Remove and drain briefly on paper towels.

5 While hot, cut the pork into thick slices. Serve on a bed of cabbage alongside cooked rice garnished with a couple of tomato slices and the parsley, and the sauces on the side for dipping.

Tip

The Tonki cooks are so careful not to disturb one crumb of the breading that they use a single bicycle spoke to move the pork from egg to panko to fryer. 'Anything thicker will ruin it,' Izuhi says, though he concedes beginners can use a spoon and their fingers.

CHAWANMUSHI
Steamed savoury egg custard

Tokyo chef Shinobu Namae calls this silky smooth chawanmushi the ultimate 'heartwarming dish'. It's a Japanese staple partnered with a French-style pheasant and clam broth – two cuisines conversing.

In culinary schools across Japan, the most popular courses of study have long been French, Italian, and Chinese cuisine. The lines between those classic cuisines and *washoku* (Japanese cuisine) were kept neatly drawn. But in the ultra-fine dining kitchen at L'Effervescence, chef Shinobu Namae is part of a new wave of Japanese chefs turning away from the strictures of classical cooking and instead looking towards pure flavour and deliciousness.

Namae began cooking professionally in an Italian pasta shop but one day came across a cookbook by the French master of modern cuisine, Michel Bras, which he says, changed his life. He would eventually cook under Bras himself in Japan and France, developing a specialty in French pastry, but he never forgot his first culinary language, the one he grew up with.

'My cooking is about the synergies of French (Western) and Japanese (Eastern) cuisines,' he says. 'I'm looking to create flavours that everyone can understand and enjoy, regardless of geography – a universal deliciousness.' The flavour combinations, which change with the seasons, are elegant yet surprising.

This chawanmushi is a dish he first learned from his mother and grandmother. At home in central Honshū, the warm custard might be garnished with toasted gingko nuts, while in Hokkaido, chestnuts are used. At his restaurant, Shinobu elevates the classic dish with a rich and savoury broth.

The ideal chawanmushi is a pillow of perfectly smooth, silky custard that melts on the tongue into pure umami. Achieving this depends, for one, on holding the cooking temperature at a steady 85°C/185°F. In other words, as with all fine cooking across the globe, the crucial ingredient is care and love.

Chef //
Shinobu Namae
Location //
L'Effervescence, Tokyo

CHAWANMUSHI
Steamed savoury egg custard

Serves 10

Preparation time: 6 hrs
Cooking time: 2½ hrs

For the shiitake dashi
80g (2¾ oz) dried shiitake mushrooms
1 litre (34 fl oz) cold water

For the katsuo-dashi
1 litre (34 fl oz) water
20g (¾ oz) kombu (ideally a delicate one,
  such as rishiri), cleaned with a damp
  tea towel
20g (¾ oz) katsuobushi (dried
  bonito flakes)

For the pheasant broth
1 tbsp vegetable oil
300g (10½ oz) pheasant, jointed, skin-on
500ml (17 fl oz) water

For the clam broth
300g (10½ oz) clams, scrubbed well
500ml (17 fl oz) water
2 tbsp kuzu (arrowroot starch), dissolved
  in 1 tbsp cold water

For the savoury egg custard
4 eggs
780–800ml (26½–27 fl oz) combined
  katsuo-shiitake dashi (see above)
1–2 tsp light soy sauce
40ml (1¼ fl oz) mirin
10g (¼ oz) salt

1 Make the shiitake dashi. Soak the dried shiitake in a large bowl of cold water for 5 hours. Remove the shiitake from the liquid, squeezing out every drop from each mushroom. Reserve the liquid.

2 Make the katsuo-dashi. Add the water to a large saucepan and place over medium heat until it reaches 65°C/150°F. Drop in the kombu, stabilise the temperature and cook for 1 hour. Remove the kombu and bring to the boil. Add the katsuobushi and take the pan off the heat immediately. Let it infuse for 1–2 minutes and then strain the dashi through a sieve lined with muslin (cheesecloth) into a bowl.

3 Next, in a jug, combine 1 litre (34 fl oz) katsuo-dashi with 200ml (7 fl oz) shiitake-dashi. Set aside.

4 Heat the oil in a deep pan over medium-high heat. Add the pheasant pieces and brown evenly all over. Add the water, making sure it is enough to cover the pheasant, and simmer over low heat for 2 hours. Pour through a sieve lined with muslin (cheesecloth) and reserve the stock.

5 Place the clams along with the water in a small saucepan and bring to the boil, just until all the shells have opened. Pour the broth through a sieve lined with muslin (cheesecloth) and reserve. (The leftover pheasant and clams can be served over rice, with a bowl of leftover broth, for lunch another day. Dashi can last for a couple months if frozen in an airtight container.)

6 Mix 400ml (13½ fl oz) pheasant broth with 100ml (3¼ fl oz) clam broth in a large saucepan. Gently bring up to a simmer, season to taste, then add the kuzu slurry. Continue to stir as the soup thickens, then remove from the heat and set aside.

7 Fill a large saucepan about 2cm (1 in) of the way up with water. Set over high heat to bring the water up to the temperature of 85–92°C/185–200°F.

8 In a bowl, whisk the eggs gently for about 10 seconds. Incorporate the katsuo-shiitake dashi by whisking it in slowly. Season with the salt, soy sauce and mirin.

9 Divide the egg mixture between ten ramekins or chawan (Japanese tea bowl) and cover each with cling film. Carefully place in the large saucepan of water, cover with a lid, and steam for 10–15 minutes, until the custard is set but the centre still jiggles slightly. Remove from the pan (careful, it will be hot) and uncover. Pour a thin layer of hot pheasant and clam broth onto the custard before serving.

BOTANIKARU IN ZA FORESUTO
Botanical in the forest

JAPONIZUMU
Japonism

These refreshing cocktails capture the essence of bar master Hiroyasu Kayama's garden in a glass. Using whatever vibrant botanicals move him, Hiroyasu creates drinks that epitomise Tokyo's sophisticated cocktail culture.

Much like tea and sake, cocktails are an integral part of the Tokyo dining experience. They arrived here in the 19th century, when Commodore Matthew Perry presented barrels of American whiskey to Emperor Meiji and his court. The pleasures of sake and shochu gave way to punch and cordials, and the Japanese bar was born.

While Prohibition slowed experimentation down across the Pacific, bartenders in Tokyo's glittering Ginza district developed novel infusions, hand-carved ice cubes, and the 'hard shake', a method of cocktail shaking used in upscale bars around the world today. Bartending became a practice of precision. Recipes were strict, even dictating how many times one should stir a Manhattan (82, to be exact).

Hiroyasu's cocktails are traditional in their meticulousness, but unlike his contemporaries', they are also improvisational. 'I'm younger than many bartenders in Japan,' he said, 'I suppose I try to be more energetic with my experimentation.'

Behind his bar, Hiroyasu often resembles a scientist more than a bartender. He distils his own absinthe from homegrown wormwood in an elaborate contraption of his own design, using techniques found in ancient French tomes. The result is a deep green liquor that tastes like a gentle, sweet, warm embrace.

Instead of rules and recipes, Hiroyasu's inspiration comes from his family farm just north of Tokyo. Lining the shelves behind his bar is a cornucopia of his harvests – anise, fennel and 'what some call weeds', he says. In the autumn, he might infuse vodka with the fragrant, young branches of *beni kaname,* a mountainous bush that tastes something like a blend of vanilla and cinnamon, and other times of the year, he might just use the bark.

For these cocktails, depending on what you have growing nearby, Hiroyasu suggests swapping in herbs such as citrusy verbena or sweet hyssop. If you don't have sudachi, another tangy citrus fruit such as lime will do. These free-spirited cocktails come from his own life, Hiroyasu says, and so they should reflect yours, too.

Owner/Bar master//
Hiroyasu Kayama
Location //
Bar Ben Fiddich, Tokyo

BOTANIKARU IN ZA FORESUTO
Botanical in the forest

Serves 1

Preparation time: 5 min

1 large ice cube
50ml (1¾ fl oz) The Botanist Islay Dry Gin,
or similar gin infused with botanicals
1 tsp Sacred Extra Dry Vermouth, or similar
spicy, dry vermouth
40ml (1¼ fl oz) bottled mineral water
small handful of assorted herbs and edible
flowers, such as soft rosemary sprigs and
flowers, fennel fronds and small mint leaves

1 Put a large ice cube in a wine glass.

2 Add the gin, vermouth and water, and vigorously swirl the glass 30 times to combine and release the aroma of the gin.

3 Garnish with the sprigs of herbs and serve straight away.

JAPONIZUMU
Japonism

Serves 1

Preparation time: 10 mins

ginger, to juice
45ml (1½ fl oz) The Botanist Islay Dry
Gin, or similar gin infused with
botanicals, chilled
20ml (¾ fl oz) sake (ideally, a crisp
daiginjo), chilled
2 tsp freshly squeezed sudachi or lime
juice, chilled
2 tsp acacia flower honey, or similar
light-flavoured honey, dissolved in 10ml
boiling water
ice cubes

1 To make the ginger juice, choose an older ginger root as the spicier the better. Use a juicer, or finely grate the ginger and squeeze through a muslin (cheesecloth) to get about 1 teaspoon juice. Put in the fridge to chill.

2 Combine the gin, sake, citrus and ginger juices, and honey in a cocktail shaker.

3 Fill the shaker with plenty of ice until the juice rises to about two-thirds full. Shake vigorously about 30 times. (Hiroyasu says, 'Put some emotion in it. Have a good time.')

4 Pour through a strainer into the glass and serve straight away.

> ## *Note*
> *Menus are rarely in English at Tokyo bars. Hiroyasu says, 'Tell us if you like whisky,*
> *gin, shochu or sake. Or better yet, say, "bartender's choice". We love to surprise you.'*

AMAZAKE
Sweet fermented rice drink

Kouichiro Kawasaki, a tenth-generation fermentation master, uses massive century-old cedar barrels for his craft, but here, he shows us how to make this nourishing sweet drink at home.

Amazake is an ancient drink made from softly sweet, fermented rice that is finding renewed interest among the health-conscious Japanese.

During the Edo period, it was common on hot summer nights to come across *furi-uri* (literally, swinging peddlers) selling amazake from buckets balanced on either end of a bamboo pole. Amazake is still made at home and served as a traditional drink for Hinamatsuri, a spring festival. Increasingly, amazake is popping up in unconventional places, from yoghurt toppings to smoothie blends. Kouichiro says you might even try it as a sweetener for cookies.

Kouichiro's family business Marukawa began in 1774 as a small rice farm in a fertile corner of Fukui Prefecture. Today, Marukawa is a miso factory, specialising in small batch organic miso and is run by Kouichiro, his sister Hiroko and brother Hironori.

Miso-making begins by mixing various combinations of grains (such as soybeans, barley and rice), with rice inoculated with the mould koji (*Aspergillus oryzae*). The koji works its magic by breaking down the starches in the grains into simple sugars. As the koji dines over weeks or months, other yeasts and bacteria join the feast. Depending on the grains, weather and time, the final results can taste assertive or mellow. Amazake is made in much the same way and involves koji and rice, left to ferment only for a day or so.

The methods for making miso and amazake in this way are laborious and exacting, and are passed down generation to generation. One of Kouichiro's first responsibilities came at age seven, when his grandfather asked him to divide up a mountain of rice into one-kilogram mounds.

'At 89, our grandfather is still at the centre of this business. He still checks on us and the operations daily,' Kouichiro says. In fact, he's the reason Marukawa makes amazake. 'He always wanted to make something sweet. He loves sweets.'

Chef //
Kouichiro Kawasaki
Location //
Marukawa Miso, Fukui

AMAZAKE
Sweet fermented rice drink

Serves 2–3 (makes about 375ml/12½ fl oz)

Preparation time: 5 mins plus 8–12 hours and 2–3 days to ferment

150ml (5 fl oz) water
150g (5½ oz) active koji (white or brown rice)

You will need: 1 litre (34 fl oz) capacity Thermos, yoghurt maker, rice cooker, or pot with immersion circulator

1 Heat the water in a large saucepan to 60°C/175°F (use a thermometer). Live koji is extremely sensitive to heat, so you may find it easiest to heat the water and then let it cool to the right temperature. If using a container that does not perfectly hold its temperature, you can start with it slightly warmer, but no higher than 70°C/160°F. Note that higher temperatures will make the amazake more sour and runny, while cooler temperatures will make it sweeter and thicker.

2 Stir the koji into the water, and then pour the mixture into your holding container. Leave to ferment at room temperature for at least 8 hours, up to 12 hours if making in winter, and give it a stir every couple of hours. After about 6 hours, use a clean spoon to taste the mixture to make sure it has not begun to turn too sour for your taste.

3 Continue to store the amazake at room temperature for 2–3 days, or refrigerate for about a week. If you heat the amazake until just barely boiling, it will keep for a month refrigerated. Drink it warm, or use it to make Amazake Ice (see below).

AMAZAKE ICE

Serves 4

Preparation time: 5 mins plus freezing

300g (10½ oz) amazake (see above)
300ml (10 fl oz) soy milk
2 tbsp plain soy yoghurt (optional)
1 tbsp kinako (roasted soy flour)
1 banana or fruit of choice, to serve

1 Combine all the ingredients in a blender and blitz until smooth.

2 Pour into a freezer-proof container, cover with the lid, and freeze for 3–4 hours. Use a fork to break up the ice every 45 minutes or so during the freeze time, or for a denser texture, after the mixture is fully frozen.

3 Serve in bowls topped with freshly sliced banana or chopped fruit of choice.

Tip

Marukawa ships koji, amazake and miso overseas via their website (in Japanese). You can also find koji at most Asian markets, though it usually comes dried. To activate it, soak in about 20 per cent of its weight in water at 38°C/100°F for a few hours and drain any excess liquid before using.

ICHIGO KAKIGORI
Strawberry shaved ice

Japan's sticky summers are inseparable from kakigori, shaved ice as frothy as cotton candy. Wajindo in Tochigi prefecture still makes it the old-fashioned way, with ice harvested the previous winter.

Kazuo Kikuchi is having an unexpectedly exciting second act. Four years ago, the 73-year-old retired architect opened a roadside stand selling kagikori in the parking lot of a farmer's market. He and his son, a graphic designer, built the clapboard structure themselves. It's now the most-popular kakigori shop in the prefecture, and draws a good many visitors from outside the region, too. On a typical sweltering summer afternoon, the line can be an hour long.

His secret? An old acquaintance who happens to be one of the few people left in Japan who produces ice the old-fashioned way: by collecting pools of mountain snowmelt and letting them freeze naturally. The ice freezes at a rate of about 1cm (½ in) per day and is harvested three times a year by cutting and hauling blocks – just like in the animated film *Frozen*.

Kazuo credits the slow freeze of the natural ice with the exceptional fluffiness of his kakigori. He also helps out with the harvesting. 'I didn't want to be one of those shops that just buys ice and serves it. Then I'd only be involved for two minutes. I want to be involved from the beginning and I want to share that experience with my customers,' he says, adding, 'I don't want the old practices to fade away.'

That said, he does use an electric machine to shave the ice, rather than an old-fashioned hand crank, which he admits would be more authentic. Many Japanese households, though they tend not to be stocked with an abundance of kitchen appliances, have classic hand-crank tabletop shavers that they take out of storage every summer.

Kakigori is sweetened with flavoured syrups and condensed milk. Wajindo's speciality is a syrup made from locally grown strawberries. Though it's a taste reminiscent of childhood, many of Wajindo's regulars are suspiciously grown up.

What sets kakigori apart from snow cones is its fluffy texture. To achieve this at home, Kazuo recommends using ice at 1°C/34°F (instead of the –10°C/14°F it is when it comes out of the freezer).

Chef //
Kazuo Kikuchi
Location //
Wajindo, Tochigi

ICHIGO KAKIGORI
Strawberry shaved ice

Serves 4

Preparation time: 15 mins
Cooking time: 4–5 mins

For the syrup
250g (9 oz) strawberries, hulled
225g (8 oz) sugar
250ml (8½ fl oz) water
½ tsp lemon juice

For the kakigori (shaved ice), per person
1.4kg (3 lb 1 oz) ice (the larger the block the better)
sweetened condensed milk (optional)

1 For the syrup, place the strawberries, sugar and water in a saucepan and bring to a boil over medium-high heat. Simmer for 4–5 minutes, to dissolve the sugar, then remove from the heat and set aside to cool completely.

2 Once cooled, blitz in a blender or food processor with the lemon juice until smooth.

3 Remove the ice from the freezer and allow it to sit at room temperature until it becomes clear instead of cloudy (this is key to achieving the fluffy texture key to this dessert).

4 To serve, add 2 tablespoons of the syrup to a bowl. Use a Japanese-style ice-shaving machine to shave one-third of the ice. Add the shaved ice to the bowl along with a further 4 tablespoons syrup and, if using, drizzle with sweetened condensed milk to taste. Repeat, finishing with a final layer of ice and serve immediately. Any remaining syrup can be stored in the freezer and defrosted for another time.

Tip
Japanese-style ice shaving machines are readily available online.

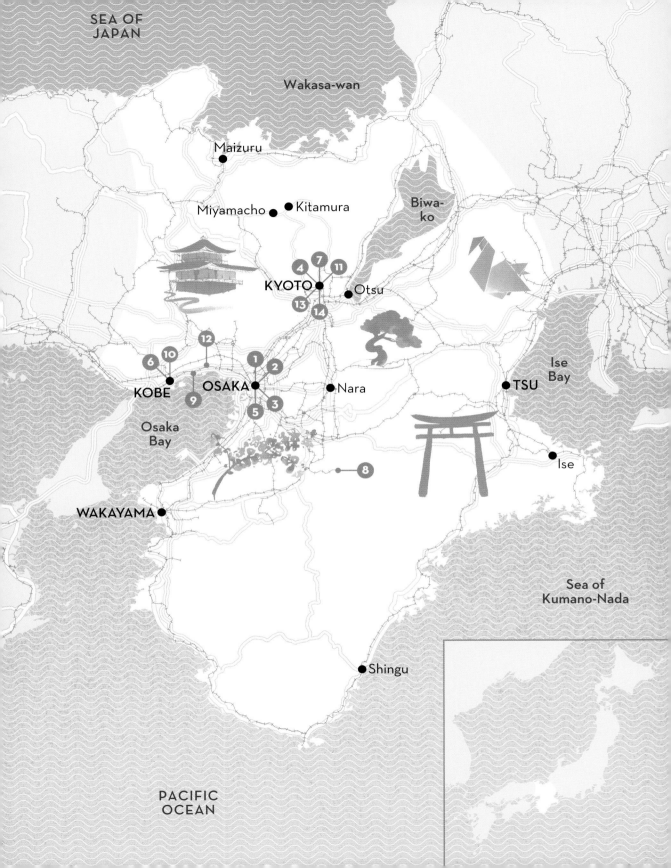

SEA OF
JAPAN

Wakasa-wan

Maizuru

Miyamacho ● ● Kitamura

Biwa-
ko

④ ⑦
KYOTO ● ⑪
● Otsu
⑬
⑭

Ise
Bay

⑫

⑥ ⑩ ① ②
KOBE OSAKA ● ● Nara ● TSU
⑨ ⑤ ③

● Ise

Osaka
Bay

⑧

WAKAYAMA ●

Sea of
Kumano-Nada

● Shingu

PACIFIC
OCEAN

KANSAI

*This region boasts both the country's most refined cuisine –
in Kyoto where imperial influences reign – and the hearty,
down-to-earth fare of merchant-founded Osaka*

TAKOYAKI
Octopus balls
page 126

OSUIMONO
The 'bowl'
page 130

KUSHIAGE
*Assorted deep-fried
skewers*
page 134

YUZUKOBOSHI
*Pickled daikon
with yuzu*
page 138

UDONSUKI
*Chicken and
clam hotpot*
page 142

GYU TAIL NO NIKOMI
Beef tail stew
page 148

SUKIYAKI
Soy-simmered beef
page 152

KAKINOHA ZUSHI
*Mackerel sushi in
persimmon leaf*
page 156

TAKOMESHI BENTO
Octopus rice
page 160

FUTOMAKIZUSHI
Thick sushi rolls
page 164

SHIPPOKU-STYLE SOBA
page 168

OHITASHI
*Braised spring
vegetables*
page 172

FU MANJU
*Steamed rice flour
dumplings with sweet
red bean paste*
page 176

KUZUKIRI
*Glass noodles
with syrup*
page 180

TAKOYAKI
Octopus balls

In Osaka, you're bound to come across takoyaki, a street snack of deep-fried batter balls on skewers. The mother of all the takoyaki stores is Aizu-ya, where 1,000 pieces a day are made.

Masaru Endo is the third-generation owner of Aizu-ya, a legendary takoyaki establishment in Osaka. She says, 'my grandfather invented this dish back when Japan was poor and there wasn't enough food for everyone. He developed a cheap, fast and delicious recipe that didn't rely on fancy ingredients. For this reason, Granddad had to research and study every day to make these seemingly unremarkable ingredients as delicious as possible.'

Ordinarily, takoyaki is enjoyed with a thick soy-mayo sauce but this is not the case at Aizu-ya where the batter has all the flavour. The key to achieving that delicious Aizu-ya taste is infusing the batter with a rich stock. The balls are crispy on the outside and fluffy inside, a testament to the skill of the chef.

Takoyaki became popular nationwide when specially designed cast-iron takoyaki pans hit the market. They say every household in Osaka has a takoyaki pan – like every household in Spain having a paella dish.

Watching takoyaki preparation at Aizu-ya is a delight. The heated pan is lashed with oil as the thin batter is poured in, followed by large chunks of octopus. The chef then takes out what looks like an ice pick and gradually and oh-so-deftly shapes each piece into a perfect sphere. The cooking of takoyaki is key, Masaru says, 'Spin those spheres around the pan, and when they are an even golden colour, it's done. If you overcook it, the batter inside becomes too chewy and then you can forget about trying to sell it...'

Pop a just-fried piece of takoyaki into your mouth and enjoy that crispy crunch followed by a smooth creamy batter. You can take-out, of course, but why not enjoy it in-store with a cold bottle of beer? At first, eat it without the sauce to see how it tastes, then maybe add some sauce later. No doubt you will understand why takoyaki are the number one street snack in Osaka.

Chef //
Masaru Endo
Location //
Aizu-ya, Osaka

TAKOYAKI
Octopus balls

Makes 24 balls

Preparation time: 10 mins
Cooking time: 15 mins

1 octopus, boiled or fresh
200g (7 oz) coarse salt (if using fresh octopus)
cooking oil, for greasing
1–2 spring onions (scallions), sliced
50g (2 oz) pickled ginger
takoyaki sauce, to serve (optional and
*   available from Asian supermarkets)*

For the batter
200g (7 oz) plain flour
3 eggs
900ml (30½ fl oz) basic dashi (page 265)
1 tbsp light soy sauce

1 Begin by rinsing the octopus under cold running water. Slice it into large pieces. Bring a pan of water to the boil and add the octopus. Cook in boiling water for about 7 minutes, then drain and allow to cool. Cut into small pieces.

2 Make the batter by putting the flour in a large bowl. Add the eggs, stock and soy sauce, and stir to create a smooth batter.

3 Lightly grease the holes in your takoyaki pan with oil and place over high heat until smoking. (Alternatively, use a Dutch pancake pan.)

4 Ladle the batter into each hole, then add the octopus, spring onions and pickled ginger. Cook for about 3 minutes, over medium-high heat, then use a wooden skewer to turn each takoyaki ball to brown all over, until golden in colour. Serve as is, or with takoyaki sauce.

OSUIMONO
The 'bowl'

The height of Japanese culinary tradition is the 'kappo' style of dining out, where customers are seated at a counter, face to face with the master, or itamae of the restaurant.

The *itamae* (master chefs) use their impressive sword-like knives behind the counter to create dishes that are works of art. And they must do everything in front of the customer's eyes. This includes prep – like gutting the fish – and all cooking and assembly. It goes without saying that mistakes are not an option, and the counter is filled with an air of concentration.

In the Funaba area of Osaka, Konoha is a highly regarded restaurant of the kappo style, whose owner, Katsumi Tanaka, is a veteran of the business. Food is served in a multiple-course format. One-by-one, the sashimi, the tempura and other delicacies appear. The main dish however is 'the bowl', or the soup course.

'The bowl' starts with a stock, usually made of dried bonito flakes and kelp, with seasonal ingredients referred to as *wantane*, or 'bowl seedlings'. The apparent simplicity belies the skill of execution and expertise of the itamae.

To eat the bowl, first lift off the lid and take in the intricate beauty of the presentation. Next, place the bowl in your hand and take a sip of the soup. The stock is considered the essence of Japanese cuisine and the quality of it really determines the skill of the itamae and the esteem of the restaurant.

Katsumi sources the ingredients at the market each day and keeps a vigilant eye on seasonal subtleties, reflecting these changes in the menu and ambience.

'Japanese cooking is based on subtraction. It's about intervening as little as possible with the ingredient, and seasonings are kept to a minimum. At the same time, one has to be creative in combinations of flavours so that it doesn't get monotonous.'

There is that feeling of happiness that rises from your stomach as you finish 'the bowl', and this is certainly one of the heights of Japanese cuisine.

Chef //
Katsumi Tanaka
Location //
Konoha, Osaka

OSUIMONO
The 'bowl'

Serves 4

Preparation time: 1 hour
Cooking time: 15 mins

1 piece 15-cm long (6 in) dried kelp (kobu)
20g (¾ oz) katsuobushi (dried bonito flakes)
50g (1¾ oz) daikon (white radish), diced
2 tsp light soy sauce
1 tsp mirin
20g (¾ oz) field mustard leaf
1 tbsp white miso
1 tsp sake
pinch of salt

1 Take a piece of kelp about 15cm (6 in) long and place in a pan along with 500ml (1 pint) cold water. Allow the kelp to soak in the water for 1 hour.

2 Place the pan over high heat and bring to the boil. Remove the kelp and add the katsuobushi. As soon as it comes to the boil again, strain and reserve the stock, and discard the katsuobushi.

3 Boil the daikon in 300ml (½ pint) of this bonito stock, seasoned with 1 teaspoon of the light soy sauce and the mirin, and cook until just tender. Boil the field mustard until wilted and then plunge into ice-cold water – this helps to keep the vivid green colour.

4 Add the white miso, sake, salt and the remaining soy sauce to the remaining 200ml (⅓ pint) stock and warm through – do not let it boil. Arrange the daikon in a serving bowl and pour over the soup. Finally, garnish with the field mustard and serve.

'The bowl is always a combination of seasonal ingredients. Spring would include bamboo shoot and red snapper, for example. It tries to convey the essence of a season. There is a tendency to combine the fruits of the sea and the mountain together in one soup.'

KUSHIAGE
Assorted deep-fried skewers

Kushiage, deep-fried skewers, are an artform in Osaka. At Wasabi, when chef Imaki Takako's delicate creations are placed on the counter, it seems almost a shame to eat them.

These popular skewers are said to have originated during the early Showa era (1920s to 1930s), when beef was very rare. Skirt steak cut from the diaphragm, usually discarded, was chopped finely and put on a skewer, then dipped in breadcrumbs and fried in lard. Owner and chef of Wasabi, Imaki Takako, has taken this traditional Osaka kushiage and from it created high-art skewers.

Imaki says, 'I aim to use seasonal ingredients as much as possible, and create food which appeals to the senses of both sight and taste. I use vegetable-based fats, and rather than meat, mostly vegetables, which can express the seasons.'

The restaurant opens at 6pm. At the counter, which seats a maximum of ten people, it's common to see young couples or diners on their own. There are always 20 types of kushiage skewers. The sauces that are served with the skewers are various interpretations of sauces from other cuisines, including Western and Chinese flavours.

Wasabi's kushiage has a fine, crunchy batter that doesn't lie heavy on the stomach, no matter how many you eat. 'In order to make the palate lighter, we include not only flour but also egg whites, egg yolks, beer, mineral water and so on in the batter. The breadcrumbs are also particularly fine. And, we try to use the minimal amount of oil when frying.'

Imaki aims to make kushiage to Japan what pinchos are to Spain. She travels regularly to Europe, and in studying wine there she made a breakthrough discovery: try savouring the piping hot kushiage together with ice-cold champagne.

Imaki's devoted efforts have led to great popularity for the restaurant, and it's being awarded the prestigious Michelin star. Customers from all over the world now visit Wasabi.

Chef //
Imaki Takako
Location //
Wasabi, Osaka

KUSHIAGE
Assorted deep-fried skewers

Makes 20 skewers

Preparation time: 15 mins
Cooking time: 10 mins

10–15 raw prawns
10 asparagus spears, cut into
    bite-sized pieces
2 small aubergines, cut into
    bite-sized cubes
vegetable oil, for deep-frying
salt
lemon wedges, to serve

For the batter
100g (3½ oz) plain flour
2 eggs, separated
20ml (½ fl oz) beer
200g (7 oz) fine breadcrumbs

You will need:
20 × 15cm (6in) bamboo skewers

1 Thread the prawns, asparagus and aubergine on to the bamboo skewers.

2 Pour enough vegetable oil in a large pan to come up to 3cm (1¼ in). Heat the oil over medium heat to 160°C/320°F (use a thermometer). (Alternatively, if a cube of bread dropped into the hot oil sizzles in 30 seconds, the oil is ready.)

3 Whisk the egg white to form firm peaks.

4 To make the batter, place the flour in a shallow bowl and add 80ml (2¾ fl oz) water and the beer. Add the egg yolk, stir until combined, then fold in the whisked egg white gently. If it seems too liquid, add a little more flour to thicken – it should have a glue-like consistency.

4 Dip the skewers into the batter and then into the breadcrumbs. Carefully slide the skewers into the hot oil and fry until cooked through and crunchy (the prawns and the asparagus will only need 2 minutes). Use tongs to remove the skewers and drain on paper towels. Season while hot with salt and serve with a wedge of lemon.

YUZUKOBOSHI
Pickled daikon with yuzu

Indispensable to the Japanese diet, tsukemono (literally, pickled things) are an essential accompaniment to rice, alcohol and even tea. The age-old means of preserving enhances the flavour of many vegetables.

The islands of Japan stretch from north to south over a range of climate zones. In addition, well-defined seasons mean a wide variety of vegetables are grown around the country throughout the year. There are said to be as many *tsukemono* (pickle) recipes around Japan as there are types of vegetables.

Kyoto is also one of the great tsukemono producing regions of Japan. Rich soils fed with abundant water from nearby rivers nourish fresh local kyo-yasai vegetables, which are then transformed into delicious pickles.

Of the numerous tsukemono specialty stores, Kintame has maintained a rich history of traditional pickling techniques since it was founded in 1887. The store shelves display around 50 different types of tsukemono, depending on the season. Tsukemono is categorised into three types according to the length of marinating: *asazuke* (lightly pickled), *fukazuke* (deeply pickled) and *chinmi* (delicacy). Lightly pickled vegetables retain a crisp texture and clear colour. Conversely, vegetables pickled for longer lose their original shape, and the flavour becomes more complex through fermentation.

Kintame's chef Masato Masuyama says, 'We create tsukemono just as a parent raises their child – with hard work and great care. At Kintame we use wooden barrels and age-old stone weights. However, mechanisation of equipment is now threatening these long-standing traditional methods.'

Kintame's top seller is *yuzukoboshi*, daikon (white radish) or turnip pickled with kombu and salt, with a citrus hit from a fruit called yuzu. Both turnip and yuzu are grown in Kyoto in winter. The light crunchy texture and addictive fresh yuzu flavour will have your stomach craving more.

Around 20 years ago, one corner of the shop was refurbished into a dining area where a full course of tsukemono can be enjoyed. The courses begin with asazuke, resembling European pickles, and continue with tsukemono sushi and a bowl of white miso. To finish, *ochazuke* (freshly steamed rice drenched in green tea) is accompanied by more tsukemono.

Chef //
Masato Masuyama
Location //
Kintame, Kyoto

YUZUKOBOSHI

Pickled daikon with yuzu

Makes 500g

**Preparation time: 5 mins plus at
least 24 hrs pickling**

700g (1½ lb) daikon (white radish) or
   turnip, peeled and sliced lengthwise
   into matchsticks
15cm (6in) piece kombu

For the pickling liquid
1 litre (34 fl oz) water
20g (¾oz) salt
50g (1¾ oz) sugar
zest and juice of 1 yuzu, zest cut into
   very fine matchsticks
30g (1 oz) sake

1 Combine the pickling liquid in a bowl and
stir to dissolve the salt and sugar.

2 Place the daikon slices and kombu in an
airtight container and pour in pickling
liquid. Seal and put a weight, equivalent to
twice the weight of the daikon, on top and
place in the fridge to pickle for between 24
hours and 3 days. The pickle can be enjoyed
after day one but it is at its prime on the
third day. Consume within a week.

UDONSUKI
Chicken and clam hotpot

Synonymous with winter in Osaka, everyone in the prefecture knows about the udonsuki served at Mimiu. Families get together and share the warming noodle hotpot during the cold months.

Udonsuki is a dish created by the restaurant Mimiu. A *nabe* (hotpot) dish, it's cooked with many additions in a dashi broth of the finest quality. Chicken, tiger prawns, clams, grilled conger eel and seasonal vegetables are simmered in the broth, with udon noodles thrown in at the end.

The most important element of the dish is the dashi broth, a fundamental and essential ingredient in Japanese cuisine. Making a fine dashi is a must-have skill for any good Japanese chef because it is this that sets each restaurant apart. The head chef of the flagship store of Mimiu, Shuichi Neya explains: 'We start making dashi at 6am. First, we put *katsuobushi* (dried bonito flakes) into boiling water, and fully extract the flavour. Katsuobushi is the main ingredient, but we also use other ingredients produced in several different areas. Then we season the broth with salt, soy sauce and a tiny amount of mirin.'

A first sip of dashi gives a very comforting, light and mellow flavour. The addition of vegetables, seafood and other ingredients infuses the dashi with richer notes.

'Guests cook udonsuki by themselves in a pot set on the table, and eat directly from it. We ask guests to relish the ingredients first, then the dashi, and lastly udon noodles cooked in the dashi. Let the udon take in all the flavours of the ingredients, and relish them. Udonsuki keeps changing its flavour from beginning to end, and so this is how you enjoy this dish.'

Udonsuki is often served at celebratory gatherings of family and friends. So much so that udonsuki kits, complete with all the ingredients needed to make the dish at home, are available to take away at Mimiu. They sell over one thousand kits a day in winter, showing just how well-loved it is by the people of Osaka.

Chef //
Shuichi Neya
Location //
Mimiu, Osaka

UDONSUKI
Chicken and clam hotpot

Serves 4

Preparation time: 20 mins
Cooking time: 30 mins

1 chicken breast, thinly sliced
8 clams, cleaned and scrubbed
4 tiger prawns
¼ head Chinese cabbage, cut into
*   bite-sized pieces*
50g (1¾ oz) carrots, cut into thin matchsticks
100g (3½ oz) tinned bamboo shoots, drained
1 bunch of chrysanthemum greens or other
*   seasonal vegetables*
8 shiitake mushrooms, sliced in half
400g (14 oz) udon noodles

For the dashi
2 litres (68 fl oz) water
400g katsuobushi (dried bonito flakes)
2–3 tsp light soy sauce
1 tsp mirin
1 tsp salt

1 To make the dashi, bring the water to the boil in a large pan. Add the katsuobushi and simmer for 2 minutes. Drain the broth in a muslin-lined sieve into a jug. Measure out 1 litre (34 fl oz) of the dashi and add the soy sauce, mirin and salt. The remaining dashi can be stored in the fridge to use another time for up to 3 days, or freeze.

2 Set up a portable gas burner and place it in the centre of the table alongside the prepared vegetables, chicken, prawns and noodles on platters (alternatively you could do this step in a saucepan on the stovetop). Pour the dashi into a heavy-based saucepan or earthen pot, and place over medium heat. Bring to a simmer, then let everyone pick their own chicken and clams from the platters and cook to their liking. Bring to the simmer again, then repeat with the vegetables. The key to delicious udonsuki is not to overcook it.

3 When all the vegetables are cooked, add the noodles to the broth and cook until al dente, then dish out the broth and noodles into each bowl. Enjoy while still hot.

GYU TAIL
NO NIKOMI
Beef tail stew

In the port city of Kōbe, Grill Mayako serves 'youshoku', or Western-style dishes. Second-generation owner, Masahiro, adapts his father's recipes (learned as a cook on a passenger ship).

Youshoku is a combination of French and other European food, adapted to match Japanese tastes (and to complement white rice, the Japanese staple). Youshoku has been developing for over 200 years, since the chefs aboard Japanese ships met their counterparts on European vessels. Pictures of these ocean-faring ships fill the walls of Grill Miyako.

One of the most iconic youshoku dishes and a specialty at Grill Miyako is beef tongue stew – tongue simmered in a demi-glace sauce. The chunks of meat are so tender that they fall apart with the gentlest brush of a fork. This rich stew is served with mashed potato, and the combination delights chef Masahiro: 'When the sauce is poured on the potato and rice, mashed up and eaten together, it is delicious. This might seem badly mannered, but as the chef, I am truly happy when people enjoy the home-made sauce that much.'

This demi-glace sauce is derived from French cuisine, and is a key base ingredient for youshoku restaurants. The old story goes that when a ship would enter port the cooks would exchange their demi-glace sauce with that of the ship docked next door. The sauce at Grill Miyako is based on the original recipe that Masahiro's father brought with him when he left the life of the sea. Masahiro says this is why the sauce isn't straightforward to replicate. 'It was inherited from my father and is a mix of the flavours of ships all around the world. Whether to pass this on or kill it is up to me. I feel that this work carries a heavily responsibility.'

In 1995, when a great earthquake hit Kōbe, the restaurant was completely destroyed. The sauce passed down from Masahiro's father was miraculously unharmed, remaining in the pot as it was. As long as Grill Miyako continues, this sauce, containing a concentrate of the efforts of many people, will also remain.

Chef //
Masahiro
Location //
Grill Miyako, Kōbe

GYU TAIL NO NIKOMI
Beef tail stew

Serves 4

Preparation time: 30 mins
Cooking time: 1 hr, plus up to 2 days to
* marinate the beef*

1kg (2 lb 3 oz) beef tail or tongue
30ml (1 fl oz) brandy
3–4 potatoes
1 tbsp single or double cream
salt and pepper
300g (10½ oz) cooked white rice (see
    page 264), to serve

For the demi-glace sauce
3 tsp cooking oil
1kg (2 lb 3 oz) beef tendons
2 onions, roughly chopped
1 celery stick, roughly chopped
1 carrot, roughly chopped
2 bay leaves
30g (1 oz) butter
40g (1½ oz) plain flour

1 Bring a large pan of water to the boil and add the beef tail. Bring back up to the boil and cook for 5 minutes, skimming off any scum that comes to the surface.

2 Carefully remove the beef tail from the pan. Allow drain and cool briefly. Heat a frying pan over high heat, rub the beef tail all over with salt and pepper and place into the hot pan. Add the brandy and let it bubble away for 5 minutes, browning the beef until the surface is crisp. Remove from the heat and set aside.

3 To make the sauce, start by heating the oil in a clean frying pan. Add the beef tendons, onions, celery, carrot and bay leaves, and cook over medium heat for 10 minutes, until the vegetables start to brown. Pour in 1 litre (34fl oz) water. Bring to the boil and simmer for 1 hour, skimming off any scum from the surface. Drain the stock into a jug.

4 Melt the butter in a saucepan and add the flour. Stir with a wooden spoon to create thick paste and cook until light brown and aromatic. Little by little, pour in up to 600ml (20 fl oz) of the beef tendon stock into the flour mixture, whisking if needed to prevent lumps. Bring to the boil and simmer for 5–10 minutes, until thickened.

5 Add the beef tail in the sauce and cook very gently for a minimum of 12 hours, or up to two days, carefully removing the scum from time to time, until the beef tail is tender. Adjust the seasoning to taste.

6 Bring a pan of water to the boil, add the potatoes and simmer until very tender. Drain, return the potatoes to the pan and mash, adding the cream and the seasoning.

7 To serve, spoon the mashed potato between plates and place the beef tail on top. Serve with rice.

SUKIYAKI
Soy-simmered beef

The Japanese love sukiyaki, where thin slices of beef, along with vegetables, are simmered at the table. In Kansai, the beef is cooked with sugar and soy sauce first.

Established in the sixth year of the Meiji Era (1873), Mishima-Tei is a famous restaurant synonymous with the Sukiyaki culture of the Kansai region. The centrepiece of sukiyaki is known as *shimo-furi*, beautifully marbled beef sirloin.

The meat eaten on a daily basis in the Kanto and Kansai regions are actually different. Diners in Kanto tend to favour pork, while in Kansai beef is supreme. There, cattle have been specially bred and reared, including 'matsuzaka gyu' and 'omi gyu', to have excellent quality to their marbling. Proprietor of Mishima-Tei, Taro Mishima's creed is to rove from place to place in order to procure top-quality beef. Taro says, 'Among 10,000 cows, there are 10,000 different flavours. The way you cut and prepare the meat differs depending on the quality of the beef you get that day. It is my job to be the connoisseur who finds only the very best beef.'

The arrival of a plate elegantly laden with beef brings shouts of glee from around the table. The meal is served in a private tatami-matted room, the meat prepared by the highly trained Mr Nakai. Customers need only focus on enjoying the food.

Mishima-Tei makes sukiyaki by heating a clay pot with a thin layer of oil, then sprinkling it with sugar. Once the sugar begins to dissolve, the beef is arranged on top. Soy-based 'warishita' sauce is poured over, and the slices are dipped into beaten egg and then enjoyed. The fullness of the egg envelops the rich umami of the marbled beef, and your mouth fills with the joy of the sumptuous beef.

First-class shimo-furi beef melts away in the mouth and anyone lucky enough to experience this outlandish sugar-dredged simmered beef will almost certainly become a repeat customer.

Chef //
Mr Nakai and
Taro Mishima (owner)
Location //
Mishima-Tei, Kyoto

SUKIYAKI
Soy-simmered beef

Serves 4

Preparation time: 5 mins
Cooking time: 10 mins

groundnut oil, for frying
20g (¾ oz) sugar
400g (14oz) high-quality marbled beef, very
thinly sliced
2 tbsp light soy sauce
1 spring onion, sliced
1 onion, sliced
1 × 200g (7oz) block fried tofu, sliced
2 eggs
2 tbsp kombu dashi (see page 265)

1 Grease a heavy-based large pan lightly with oil and place over medium-high heat. Sprinkle the sugar into the pan and continue to heat until it begins to dissolve. Arrange the slices of beef, fatty side down, in one layer. Pour over the soy sauce and let it bubble and brown.

2 Beat the eggs in a bowl and when the beef starts to brown, use chopsticks to remove the slices from the pan, reserving the juices in the pan. Dip the beef into the egg swiftly and remove.

3 Heat the same pan used for the beef. Add the spring onion, onion and tofu, then let simmer in the sweetened soy juices for 5–7 minutes. If a little dry or if the flavour is too strong, add the dashi.

'Really top-class beef is sweet, and melts
in the mouth. While the beef itself is
delicious, so too are the onions and tofu
that soak up the umami flavour.'

KAKINOHA ZUSHI
Mackerel sushi
in persimmon leaf

*A representative
delicacy of
Yoshino in the
Nara Prefecture,
kakinoha zushi
is a variety of
sushi wrapped in
persimmon leaves
with intriguing
origins.*

Tourists flock to Nara Prefecture, located next to Kyoto and Osaka, to see the oldest Buddhist temples in Japan – such as the Great Buddha of Nara – and the cherry blossom, the national flower of Japan. Within the prefecture, the mountain village Yoshino is famous for the *sakura* (cherry blossom), where in spring, thousands of cherry trees burst into bloom at once on the slopes, and the stunning scenery is described as the original landscape of the Japanese heart.

Hirasou, situated in Yoshino, is a long-established Kakinoha zushi store, with a history spanning 150 years, and is well-known nationwide. But, how did sushi, made with fresh seawater fish, become a delicacy of the land-locked Nara Prefecture? Hirasou was originally a *ryokan* (traditional Japanese inn) that served meals cooked with mountain vegetables and freshwater river fish. Kakinoha zushi was only made at home, but during the mid-Edo period, Hirasou began serving it as a delicacy to guests during the summer festival and this gained popularity in the area.

The owner of Hirasou, Sousuke Hirai, explains the origins of kakinoha zushi: 'The fish, *saba* (mackerel) is caught in the Kumanonada Sea, 50km from Nara. In the olden days, when there was no electricity or refrigeration, peddlers preserved saba with salt so it could be transported over the mountains. The saba was then paired with locally produced rice and made into sushi.' Saba became an important source of protein for people living in the mountainous area of Yoshino, and the popularity of kakinoha zushi spread quickly. However, sushi made from fish went off quickly in summer, so the people of Yoshino set their sights on persimmon leaves. 'The tannins contained in persimmon leaves have an antiseptic effect. By wrapping the sushi in persimmon leaves, it could be kept fresher longer. The leaves also made it easier to carry the sushi.' All of which created a unique food culture. Nowadays although various kinds of seafood are used for kakinoha zushi, the tradition of wrapping the sushi with persimmon leaves has remained.

Chef //
Sousuke Hirai
Location //
Hirasou, Nara

KAKINOHA ZUSHI
Mackerel sushi in persimmon leaf

Serves 4

Preparation time: 2¾ hrs
Cooking time: 5 mins plus rice cooking

15cm (6in) kombu
20–25 persimmon leaves

For the fish
1 fresh saba (mackerel) fillet
salt, for sprinkling
110–165ml (4–5½ fl oz) rice vinegar

For the sushi rice
360g (12½ oz) cooked short-grain rice
 (see page 264)
45ml (1½ fl oz) rice vinegar
40g (1½ oz) sugar
½ tsp salt

1 Sprinkle the fish fillet with plenty of salt, cover and leave to sit for 1 hour.

2 Meanwhile, prepare the sushi rice. Heat the rice vinegar, sugar and salt in a small saucepan, stirring to dissolve the sugar. Remove from the heat and set aside to cool.

3 As soon as the rice is cooked, transfer to a large bowl. Gradually add the sushi vinegar and use a spatula to turn the rice, allowing it to cool until almost at room temperature.

4 Rinse the fish under cold running water to rid of the salt and put in the bowl and pour over enough vinegar to cover, making sure the fish is submerged. Leave to pickle for 15 minutes.

5 The surface of the fish should now be white in colour; remove from the vinegar and use a sharp knife to help peel the skin away from the flesh. Cut the fish on the diagonal into thin slices.

6 Dip your hands into a bowl of water– this prevents sticking. Take a small amount of sushi rice, about 1 tablespoon, in one hand. Using a few quick motions shape into a ball being careful not to squeeze too firmly but firm enough for it to keep its shape. Place on top of a persimmon leaf, put the fish slices top of the rice ball and wrap. Repeat until done and leave the sushi to stand in a cool place for 1 hour before eating.

'Fish represents the God of the ocean, rice represents the God of the earth, and leaves represent the God of the mountains. Eating kakinoha zushi at a summer festival is a way to express our gratitude and respect to nature. Kakinoha zushi is a symbol of nature-loving Japanese, which I hope to pass on to the next generations.'

TAKOMESHI BENTO
Octopus rice

These lunch boxes were created to mark the opening of the Akaishi Kaikyo Bridge in 1995. Their unique shape and the taste of the local octopus have made them famous.

The Akaishi Kaikyo Bridge, connecting the islands of Honshu and Shikoku, is the world's longest at 3900m. The Akaishi Strait lies beneath it, and is known as one of the main fishing grounds of the Kansai region.

The octopus known as *Akaishi tako* is of a particularly high class. The Akaishi *takomeshi bento*, or octopus rice lunch box, is famous throughout Japan (even amongst the endless varieties of lunch boxes) as one of the most delicious. And one of the prettiest, too: the container in which the meal is served is unique, created in the image of the *takotsubo*, the pot used when catching octopus.

Yanagimoto Yuki, who makes these takomeshi bento at the restaurant Awajiya in Akaishi, explains: 'Octopus become active at night and hunt for shrimp and crabs. When the octopus is full, it has the habit of diving into dark, narrow spaces such as under rocks or in the shade of driftwood. In Akaishi, the takotsubo pots are laid at the bottom of the ocean, and octopus are caught after they enter them.'

When you open the lid of the takotsubo container, you are greeted by large chunks of sweetly boiled octopus, and vegetables cooked in the juices. Under this is a bed of rice, cooked in an octopus dashi.

'Octopus is a food which is just great chunks of umami flavour. First of all you can enjoy the texture of the octopus chunks, then enjoy it together with the rice, which has absorbed all the umami of the octopus. Whenever people taste it for the first time, they are surprised at how rich the umami flavours of the octopus are.'

Awajiya first made this dish as a train station lunch box, to be eaten while travelling. For this reason, the delicacy is carefully balanced to be at its best not just when it is freshly cooked but also when cold. The taste to be enjoyed after purchasing one of these takomeshi bento at Akaishi Station, and again while gazing out at the calm seas from the train windows, is really something special.

Chef //
Yanagimoto Yuki
Location //
Awajiya, Kōbe

TAKOMESHI BENTO
Octopus rice

Serves 4

Preparation time: 20 minutes
Cooking time: 20 minutes

360g (12½ oz) rice
500g (1 lb 2 oz) octopus, raw
1 tbsp soy sauce
1 tbsp mirin
1 tbsp sugar
40g (1½ oz) tinned bamboo shoots, cut
   into bite-sized cubes
15g (½ oz) carrot, cut into bite-sized
   chunks
10g (¼ oz) sugarsnap peas
360ml (12 fl oz) kombu dashi (see page 265)

1   Wash the rice and place in a bowl of water to soak for at least 30 minutes.

2   Bring a pan of water to the boil and add the octopus. Blanch for 7–10 minutes, then drain, reserving a tablespoon of the liquid.

3   Take half of the boiled octopus, roughly chop and set aside. Cut the remaining octopus into bite-sized chunks and place in a saucepan with just enough water to cover. Add the soy sauce, mirin and sugar. Throw in the bamboo shoots and carrot and simmer over a low heat for 10 minutes, or until about 100ml (3½ oz) remains.

4   Rinse and drain the rice. Roughly chop the reserved boiled octopus and then put into a food processor and blitz into fine pieces. Put the rice and octopus paste into a rice cooker, and pour over the kombu dashi. Add 1 tablespoon of the liquid from cooking the octopus, and set the rice to cook. (If you don't have a rice cooker, do this step in a saucepan with a tight-fitting lid for about 20 minutes, until tender.)

5   Blanch the sugarsnap peas in a pan of salted water for 2 minutes. Drain.

6   Once the rice is ready, scoop into a bento-style container (or lunch box) and top with the octopus chunks, bamboo shoots and carrot. Garnish with the sugarsnap peas.

FUTOMA KIZUSHI
Thick sushi rolls

Makizushi rolls from Higaki are often bought as gifts for loved ones. This is because each day, Tomoaki Higaki puts all his concentration into every piece he makes.

Sushi rolls, or *makizushi*, are made by spreading sushi rice over toasted nori seaweed, topping with any of your favourite ingredients, and rolling it all in a bamboo mat. While easily made at home, there is one particular restaurant which must be mentioned when talking about what real makizushi is.

The restaurant is Higaki in the port city of Kōbe. On a busy day, they will sell 200 sushi rolls. They're a popular gift to bring to friends or family. These gift rolls have traditionally been wrapped in a bamboo sheath. As well as absorbing just the right amount of water, the bamboo is said to have antibacterial effects.

The owner who rolls the sushi himself, Higaki Tomoaki, was actually a 'salaryman' until he was 35. He trained as a sushi chef, and eventually was able to open his own place.

'At first, I was just trying to watch, and was not able to roll beautiful sushi myself. It was all I could do just to keep up with the numbers. Only after ten years was I able to start rolling futomaki that I could be satisfied with.'

Mr Higaki rolls sushi like a master. First, he places the vinegared rice on the nori, followed by the homemade *atsuyaki tamago* omelette, *fukumeni* made with sweet-and-sour cooked shiitake, and *mitsuba* (trefoil) or other greens for garnish. He then rolls them at once, with one breath. Without measuring, he slices the sushi into eight pieces, certainly and swiftly. The cut surfaces are beautifully straight, and every piece is exactly the same thickness.

'When making makizushi, I consider the firmness of that day's rice, and change how much strength I put in little by little accordingly. You must never push it too strongly. It is ideal if when eaten, each individual grain of rice can be felt as you hold it, and then the rice delicately collapses in your mouth.'

While delicious fresh, the makizushi also have a wonderful flavour when you eat them a little later, when the flavour of the ingredients within has spread to the rice.

Chef //
Higaki Tomoaki
Location //
Higaki, Kōbe

FUTOMAKIZUSHI
Thick sushi rolls

Serves 4

Preparation time: 1 hr
Cooking time: 20 mins

4 sheets nori seaweed
360g (12½ oz) short-grain rice
10cm (4 in) sheet kombu
bunch of mitsuba (Japanese parsley) or a
 handful of green beans

For the sushi vinegar
80ml (2½ fl oz) rice vinegar
60g (2 oz) sugar
5g (¼ oz) salt

For the shiitake mushrooms
6 dried shiitake mushrooms
100ml (3½ fl oz) water
45g (1½ oz) sugar
45g (1½ oz) soy sauce

For the omelette
3 eggs
1 tbsp sake
30g (1¼ oz) sugar
5g (¼ oz) salt
cooking oil, for frying

1 Make the sushi rice. Wash the rice well in water, put in a bowl and cover with plenty of water. Allow to soak for 30 minutes, then drain.

2 Place the rice and 360ml (12 fl oz) of water in the rice cooker, place the kombu on top and cook (if you don't have a rice cooker, simply place in a tight-fitting pan and simmer for about 20 minutes until the rice is tender).

3 Soak the dried shiitake mushrooms for 15 minutes. Meanwhile, heat the rice vinegar, sugar and salt in a small saucepan, stirring to dissolve the sugar. Remove from the heat and set aside to cool.

4 As soon as the rice is cooked, transfer to a large bowl. Gradually add the sushi vinegar and use a spatula to turn the rice, allowing it to cool until almost at room temperature.

5 Place the shiitake in a saucepan along with the water, sugar and soy sauce. Set over medium heat and simmer until the liquid has evaporated, about 10 minutes. Be careful not to let it burn. Take off the heat and leave to cool, then slice the shiitake into thin strips.

6 To make the omelette, whisk the eggs with sake, sugar and salt. Heat a little oil in a tamago-yakiki (a rectangular pan for making Japanese omelettes), or a non-stick frying pan, over a medium-high heat. When hot, add a ladleful of the egg mixture to the pan, just enough to make a thin, even layer. Wait a few seconds for the egg to begin to set, then use a pair of chopsticks to roll the omelette into a log towards the other end of the pan. Add a bit more oil, then another ladleful of the egg mixture, tilting the pan to coat. Wait a few seconds and then roll the log back to the other end of the pan. Repeat until all the egg is cooked.

7 Trim the ends off the omelettes, then slice into thin ribbons. Set aside.

8 Blanch the mitsuba in a pan of salted boiling water very briefly, then remove and drain.

9 Place a nori sheet on a makisu sushi mat, and evenly spread the sushi rice on top, followed by the egg strips, shiitake and mitsuba. Roll firmly, using the mat, and making sure that the vegetables are contained. Leave to sit for 15–30 minutes so that the flavours can mingle, then cut into bite-sized slices.

SHIPPOKU-STYLE SOBA

It is said in Japan that Kanto in the east is soba, and Kansai in the west is udon. However, in Kyoto a particular local soba culture has developed.

Owariya in Kyoto, which was established 550 years ago, was first founded as a sweets store. Soba restaurants in Kanto in eastern Japan were always an ordinary person's fast food which developed from street stalls, but this was not the case in Kyoto. At Zen temples, soba was called *tenshin*, and was a snack to be eaten when peckish. Owariya has a deep connection with these Zen temples, and began to sell sweets made from soba, or buckwheat, flour. As time passed, it gradually became a soba restaurant. Masu Okamoto of Owariya says: 'There are various foods in Kyoto which are supported by the water quality such as tofu and yuba, but the top of the list is certainly dashi.'

Dashi is said to be the heart of Kyoto cuisine, and for this, kombu seaweed from Hokkaido is crucial. This, together with a mix of various kinds of bonito flakes known as katsuobushi, are used to make a unique dashi. Masu is particular about the water he uses for dashi.

'We use this groundwater not only for the dashi, but also when we make and boil the soba noodles. This means that the soba is smooth, and yet has a chewy texture, making delicious noodles,' says Masu.

There are various famous items on the Owariya menu, but particularly tasty is the Shippoku soba. 'Shippoku' means a dish with various different kinds of ingredients piled together on the same plate. So just as in the name, this dish features a plate with warm dashi and freshly boiled soba, topped with a thin egg omelette, kamaboko fish sausage, shiitake, and colourful green vegetables.

When you first take a mouthful of the dashi, the umami flavour of the kombu and the fragrance of the bonito flakes hit you. The soba is smooth and, eaten in turns with the vegetables, will not last long.

The restaurant also features various other items on the menu, including of course, in true Kansai style, udon.

Chef //
Masu Okamoto
Location //
Owariya, Kyoto

SHIPPOKU-STYLE SOBA

Serves 4

Preparation time: 8 hrs
Cooking time: 15 mins

20cm (8 in) sheet kombu
30g (1 oz) katsuobushi (dried bonito flakes)
1 tsp soy sauce
1 tsp mirin
200g (7 oz) dried soba noodles
1 egg
pinch of salt
cooking oil, for frying
5cm (2 in) piece kamaboko fish paste,
*   cut into 5mm (¼ in) slices*
20g (¾ oz) spinach leaves

1 Pour 1 litre (1¾ pints) water into a saucepan and add the kombu. Leave to sit for 8 hours for the flavour to infuse.

2 Set the pan with the kombu and water over a high heat and bring to the boil. Remove the kombu with a slotted spoon and add the katsuobushi. Leave to steep for about 1 minute, then strain the broth through a fine sieve into a jug. Return to the pan along with the soy sauce and mirin and simmer over a very low heat while you prepare the remaining elements.

3 Make the omelette by beating the egg with a pinch of salt. Heat a frying pan with a little oil and add the egg, tilting the pan to form an even layer over the surface. Take off the heat once cooked, and thinly slice.

4 Bring a pan of salted water to the boil and blanch the spinach for 1 minute. Drain and plunge into a bowl of ice-cold water and drain again. Roughly chop.

5 Fill a pan with fresh water and bring to the boil. Add the soba noodles and cook according to the packet instructions or for about 2–4 minutes, until tender to the bite. Drain and rinse under cold water.

6 Warm your serving bowls. Divide the noodles between bowls and ladle over the hot broth. Garnish with the egg, kamaboko and spinach.

OHITASHI
Braised spring vegetables

The simplicity of ohitashi – boiled vegetables in dashi – is deceptive. To get the most from your ingredients, you must know a great deal about the delicacies of each season.

One stop on the rapid train from Kyoto, in a quiet residential area, lies Kyo-Ryori Takagi. As you enter, bowing under the noren curtain, decorated according to the season, you are greeted by a beautiful, simple interior in a modern Japanese style. The owner, Kazuo Takagi, displaying his skills in the centre of the counter, is one of the young flag-bearers of Japanese cuisine.

Kazuo explains, 'Japanese cuisine is not like Western food which is about adding a variety of different complementary tastes; rather, it is what we can call "the cuisine of subtraction", which removes excess cooking in order to bring out the natural flavours of the ingredients as much as possible.'

The *ohitashi* made by Mr Takagi involves one of the oldest methods of preparing food in Japan. The verb *hitasu* means to immerse or soak, and that's what they do. The quickly boiled seasonal vegetables are placed to soak in a dashi stock known as *suiji*.

'Western style salads feature raw vegetables eaten with an oily dressing; however, in Japan, we do not use such oil. Instead, we place boiled vegetables to soak in suiji, which complements the umami flavours and takes out the acrid bitterness of the vegetables.'

Any seasonal vegetable can be used. In spring, mountain vegetables grown on the hills after the snow melts are the key player.

'Various kinds of vegetables are flavoured in the same suiji, yet the flavouring is extremely light. By keeping it so light, this actually means that the unique taste of each vegetable can be clearly and individually enjoyed.'

It's important that the vegetables are not over-boiled, as that destroys their fragrances and textures. There may be only a few steps in the preparation, but perfection takes serious professional skill.

Kazuo is involved in a reform of meals provided at schools throughout Japan, based on his mission to ensure that children understand the refined flavours of Japanese cuisine even from a young age.

Chef //
Kazuo Takagi
Location //
Kyo-Ryori Takagi, Hyōgo

OHITASHI
Braised spring vegetables

Serves 4

Preparation time: 5 mins
Cooking time: 5 mins

2 tsp salt
500–700g (1 lb 2 oz) seasonal spring
*   vegetables (such as nanoha, urui or udo;*
*   alternatively, replace with any crunchy*
*   spring vegetables that have a bitterness*
*   when raw, such as carrots or sugarsnap*
*   peas)*

For the suiji broth
100ml (3½ fl oz) katsuo dashi (see page 265)
1 tsp light soy sauce
1 tsp mirin

1 Bring a large pan of water and the salt to the boil.

2 Add the spring vegetables, cooking each vegetable separately, and blanch them for 20–30 seconds. Be careful not to overcook them otherwise the texture and flavour will be ruined.

3 Drain and then plunge the vegetables into a bowl of ice-cold water (this helps to retain the vibrant colour of the vegetables). Drain, then put on top of paper towels to remove excess water.

4 Mix together the suiji broth ingredients.

5 Transfer the vegetables to a large bowl. Pour the suiji broth over and leave to sit for 5–10 minutes, then serve.

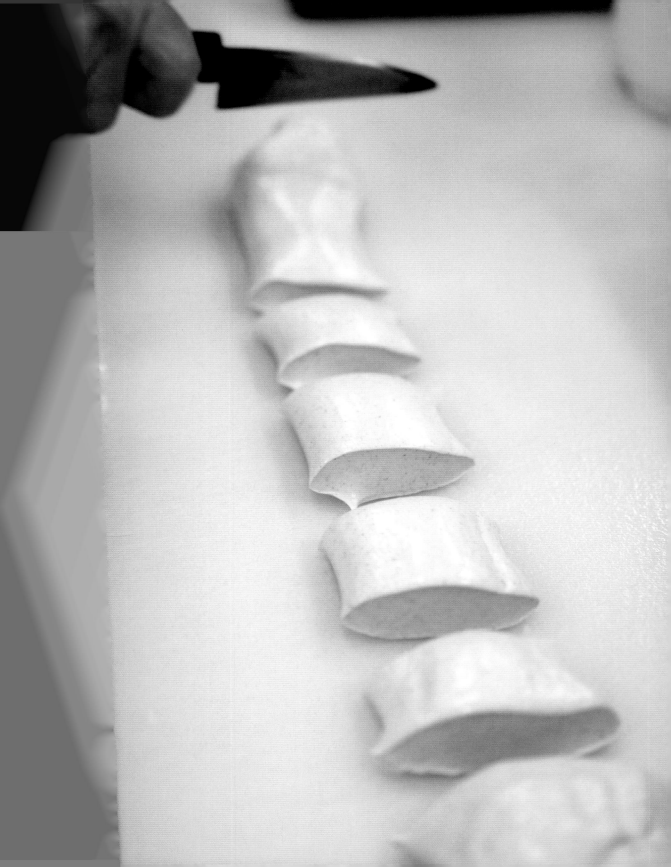

FU MANJU
Steamed rice flour dumplings with sweet red bean paste

Pop one of these sweet dumplings in your mouth and savour the sumptuous texture that is at once thick and springy. Real fu is the only way to achieve this texture.

Traditional Japanese *shojin* cuisine is based on Buddhist principles, chiefly non-violence and the consequent avoidance of animal products. Today, the cuisine has become popular with vegetarians. Many foods we see in Japanese supermarkets such as tofu, aburaage and yuba actually have their origins in shojin cuisine. Protein-rich soybeans were chosen as an alternative to supplement the vegetarian diet, which lacked sufficient protein for proper growth.

With its numerous temples, Kyoto has long been a centre of shojin cuisine. A shojin food made of wheat gluten known as *fu* is one of many foods developed here for its resemblance to meat. While it has little flavour on its own, when soaked in a fine dashi broth, it becomes an indispensable ingredient in Kyoto cuisine. The texture changes with different preparation methods, and can be enjoyed grilled, braised or in soups. Its versatility makes it adaptable for any type of cooking, and is only limited by the imagination.

For 200 years, fu specialist Fuka has produced this staple of shojin cuisine. One of their popular items is 'fu-manju'. Containing fresh fu with azuki (red bean) paste wrapped in bamboo leaves, deliciously springy and silky, it has become one of the most popular Kyoto gifts.

Fuka's Shuichiro Kohori says, 'We combine gluten and sticky mochi rice two parts to one and steam it quickly. It's important to get a firm, jelly-like texture. The whole process is done by hand, so there is no way to mass produce them.'

In order to promote this delicacy abroad, Fuka have developed new products in addition to fu-manju and using ingredients that translate to French or Italian cuisine such as basil and tomato paste. This sweet recipe came to Japan 500 years ago from mainland Asia and is once again captivating the public.

Chef //
Shuichiro Kohori
Location //
Fuka, 413 Higashi
Uratsuji-Cho, Kyoto

FU MANJU

*Steamed rice flour dumplings
with sweet red bean paste*

Makes 15–20 dumplings

**Preparation time: 3¾ hrs plus
  overnight soaking**
Cooking time: 35 mins

150g (5½ oz) strong white flour
10g (¼ oz) salt
40g (1½ oz) rice flour (shiratama)
25g (1 oz) yomogi (wormwood), optional
10g (¼ oz) mizuame starch syrup

For the azuki bean paste
150g (5½ oz) azuki red beans
150g (5½ oz) sugar

1 Put the beans in a large bowl, cover with plenty of cold water and leave to soak overnight.

2 Drain the beans, then rinse well and drain. Transfer to a large saucepan with about 5–6 times more water than the quantity of beans. Bring the boil, then reduce the heat to a simmer, cover and cook for about 1½–2 hours, or until the beans are soft. Top up the water if necessary to keep the beans covered in water at all times. Add the sugar and cook, uncovered for a further 45 minutes, stirring occasionally. Turn off the heat when the mixture has become paste-like. Leave to cool. The bean paste will keep for a week in the fridge, or freeze for up to 3 months.

3 Meanwhile, prepare the dumplings by placing the flour, salt and 100ml (3½ fl oz) water in a large bowl. Mix, then leave to sit for approximately 2 hours, until the mixture becomes dough-like and the texture of an earlobe.

4 If using yomogi, place it in boiling water for 30–60 seconds. Remove and submerge immediately in cold water to retain its vivid colour.

5 Fill a sink with cold water. Transfer the dough to a clean tea towel, wrap tightly and knead in the cold water repeatedly, changing the water often, until the water remains clear. Set the dough aside, then scrape the light brown sticky residue (gluten) from the tea towel and set aside for 1 hour. Then mix it with the shiratama powder, boiled yomogi (if using) and mizuame, until this is also the texture of an earlobe.

5 Divide the dough into bite-sized pieces and mould into rounds. Arrange in a single layer in a steamer and steam for 10 minutes. Repeat with the remaining dumplings, if needed.

6 To serve, arrange on a plate and top with the azuki bean paste.

KUZUKIRI
Glass noodles with syrup

There's a peculiar food in this world called kuzukiri. It has been passed down over 300 years and 15 generations as a traditional sweet in Kyoto, by the restaurant Kagizen.

Kagizen has a long relationship with the entertainment districts, where kimono-clad women known as *maiko-san* would perform songs and dances to brighten parties. Gion is known even today as the most refined of such areas within Kyoto, and Kagizen is located behind a noren curtain within Gion itself.

Kuzukiri is one of the much-loved treats of the entertainment area. It is made by dissolving the starch from the roots of a plant known as the kuzu (also known as 'kudzu', arrowroot starch) in water. The highest quality kuzu is made by picking apart the fine threats of the root at the most severe peak of winter, purifying it by washing it several times in groundwater, and then drying it naturally.

When the dried kuzu dissolves, the water becomes cloudy. At Kagizen, this is then poured into a bronze pot and double-boiled. Once the cloudiness clears and it starts to solidify, it's sliced into noodle-like lengths. These are then dipped into a sugar syrup to eat. The silky smooth texture cannot be replicated in anything other than kuzukiri.

Hamano Koji of Kagizen Ryobo says: 'This is eaten with non-slippery wooden chopsticks just like udon noodles. This is so that the lipstick and kimono of the white-painted geiko will not be spoiled. The deliciousness of kuzukiri is best enjoyed while fresh. Slurping down these smooth, cold strips dipped in sweet syrup is something familiar to all in Kyoto, even today.'

Due to its simplicity, kuzukiri also has great depths. Of particularly importance is the water. The taste of kuzukiri is particular to Kyoto, where low-calcium water flows naturally and abundantly. According to Koji, Kagizen once used well water, but now is able to use high-quality water from the tap.

It is said in Kyoto that a restaurant needs to exist for 300 years before it can be referred to as a 'long-established business'. The people of Kyoto have continuously loved kuzukiri over all of these years. If you enjoy it together with rich matcha, you too can become lost in the taste of 300 years of history in Kyoto.

Chef //
Hamano Koji
Location //
Kagizen Ryobo, Kyōto

KUZUKIRI
Glass noodles with syrup

Serves 4

Preparation time: 5 mins
Cooking time: 15 mins

30g (1 oz) soft light brown sugar
30g (1 oz) granulated sugar
100g (3½ oz) kuzu (arrowroot starch)

1 Put both sugars to a saucepan and place over low heat. Allow to melt, without stirring or moving the pan, until dark brown in colour, then turn off the heat. Be careful not to let the syrup burn.

2 In a bowl, combine the kuzu with 250ml (8½ fl oz) water. Mix thoroughly. Pour through a fine strainer to ensure that there are no lumps.

3 Pour a ladleful of the kuzu mixture into a wide pan on a high heat, tilting the pan to coat the surface with the mixture. Bring to the boil, then reduce the heat to medium. Allow to cook for 2 minutes until translucent. Remove immediately from the heat and use a fish slice to carefully remove the layer from the pan. Slide into a bowl of ice-cold water and let it cool completely. Repeat until all the kuzu mixture is cooked.

4 Drain and then cut the kuzu into thin strips with a knife. To eat, dip the noodles into the syrup. The easiest way to eat them is to use wet wooden chopsticks – this stops them from sliding around too much.

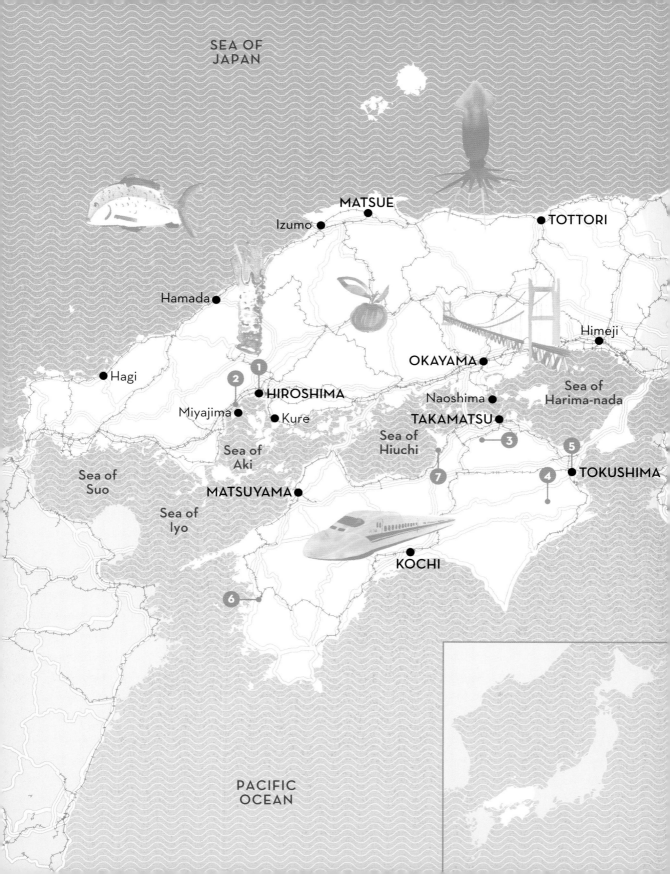

SEA OF
JAPAN

MATSUE

Izumo

TOTTORI

Hamada

Himeji

Hagi

OKAYAMA

1

2

HIROSHIMA

Naoshima

Sea of
Harima-nada

Miyajima

Kure

TAKAMATSU

Sea of Aki

Sea of
Hiuchi

3

5

Sea of
Suo

MATSUYAMA

7

4

TOKUSHIMA

Sea of
Iyo

KOCHI

6

PACIFIC
OCEAN

WESTERN JAPAN

Surrounded by two seas, this region is known for fresh fish all year round. Rice and vegetables are abundant due to the moderate climate; dishes here are sweet and flavourful

OKONOMIYAKI
Savoury pancake

It is rare to meet someone who does not like okonomiyaki – the popular savoury Japanese pancake found all over Japan.

Hiroshima is famous for okonomiyaki. Walking through the town, you will be greeted with the aromas of the pancake grill. These savoury pancakes vary throughout regions in Japan, but in Hiroshima they consist of a very thin layer of crisp batter topped with heaps of finely cut cabbage, beansprouts and strips of pork belly. *Okonomi* means 'as you like', which is fitting as the pancakes are either grilled or fried on a hot iron plate and your choice of finishing touches include the sweet and salty okonomiyaki sauce, dried nori seaweed, *katsuobushi* (dried bonito flakes) and/or lashings of mayonnaise.

Of all the restaurants in Hiroshima, Mitchan is considered the original. It first began in 1950 as a street stall, the style which subsequently spread throughout Japan. 'The city of Hiroshima was completely destroyed by the atomic bomb during World War II,' explains Manabu Uekawa of Mitchan. 'During the impoverished post-war era, okonomiyaki kept people's stomachs full.'

Okonomiyaki is traditionally eaten not with chopsticks but with a small metal fish slice-like utensil known as a *hera*. Using a *hera* instead of chopsticks to eat okonomiyaki actually began at the Mitchan stall, as the owner wanted to save on washing up. This frugality mirrors the ingredients in the pancake – Manabu says, 'The idea of adding beansprouts to the cabbage came about as a last resort measure by the owner when cabbage was very expensive due to bad weather conditions. Adding beansprouts also increases the volume, and gives a crunchy texture.'

Okonomiyaki might be cooked on a hot plate, but the ingredients are partly steamed. As the cabbage and bean sprouts are slowly fried, they produce water that steams these and the other ingredients. When you bite into a piping hot mouthful, the seasoned pork, concentrated sweetness of the cabbage, and rich sauce mix together in your mouth, creating a complex and evocative flavour.

Chef //
Manabu Uekawa
Location //
Mitchan, Hiroshima

OKONOMIYAKI
Savoury pancake

Makes 2

Preparation time: 5 mins
Cooking time: 10 mins

cooking oil, for frying
150g (5 oz) plain flour
200g (7 oz) head cabbage, thinly shredded
40g (1½ oz) bean sprouts
6 pieces pork belly, thinly sliced
1 egg
salt and pepper

To serve
okonomiyaki sauce (if unavailable,
   mix 3 parts Worcestershire sauce
   with 1 part ketchup)
dried nori seaweed flakes
katsuobushi (dried bonito flakes)
mayonnaise

1 Heat a thin layer of oil in a large frying pan over medium heat. In a bowl, combine the flour with 250ml (8½ fl oz) water and seasoning. Add a small ladleful of the batter into the pan, tilting to form a very thin layer.

2 Put the cabbage, bean sprouts and pork slices on top and use a *hera* or fish slice to gently turn over, pushing down with the flat side of the *hera* or fish slice. Push the pancake towards the side of the pan and allow to cook over medium-low heat for about 10 minutes.

3 Crack the egg into the space in the pan and fry until partially cooked, place it on top of the pancake, then flip over once more.

4 Drizzle with okonomiyaki sauce, nori flakes, katsuobushi and generously squirt over the mayonnaise. Chop into pieces and enjoy.

'The city of Hiroshima was completely destroyed by the atomic bomb during World War II. During the impoverished post-war era, okonomiyaki kept people's stomachs full.'

ANAGO MESHI

Grilled conger eel with rice for bento

The numbers of conger eels (anago) in Japanese seas are declining. Get to Hiroshima and join the waiting list for Ueno's transcendent anago and rice bento.

The Japanese 'bento' or lunch-box culture is popular around the world. Any kind of food can be placed in a bento, but there is a strict condition that it should still taste good even when it's cold. In that sense, the *anago meshi* (conger eel rice) from Ueno in Hiroshima can be said to be the king of bentos – it is particularly delicious cold.

Ueno began to sell anago meshi there around one hundred years ago. According to current owner Mr Ueno, 'Anago can be caught all year round in the Seto Inland Sea. Anago meshi began when we started to sell lunch boxes containing char-broiled anago placed on top of rice cooked in the broth taken from the bones of the anago itself.'

When you open up the traditional wooden bento box, known as *kyogi*, you will see lines of anago slivers cut at 45-degree angles. The only accompaniment is pickles, and this simplicity makes the dish. The sweet sauce on the grilled eel and the rice containing the flavours of the anago itself combine, and it is difficult to stop eating.

Mr Ueno explains, 'We only use what is known as *ike anago*, which is where after being caught the eel is kept alive overnight in a tank of water to clean it, and then cut and gutted. This is then grilled, pure and simple. The fatty anago just falls to pieces in your mouth.'

In recent years the anago catch has rapidly decreased, and it has become very difficult to obtain high-quality anago. Because this dish is just char-grilled, its taste depends on the anago itself. There is no room for compromise. Due to the limited number of quality eels available, fewer bento boxes are made.

When asked the secret of being tasty even when cold, Mr Ueno responds, 'Freshly grilled anago, and freshly cooked rice. These are both placed in the bento box while they are still hot. Because the box is made from wood, the unnecessary liquid is let out, and only the flavours and umami are trapped inside. That is the secret.'

Chef //
Mr Ueno
Location //
Ueno, Hiroshima

ANAGO MESHI

Grilled conger eel with rice for bento

Serves 4

Preparation time: 1 hr
Cooking time: 1 hr

2 anago (conger eels)
300g (10½ oz) short-grain white rice
300ml (10 fl oz) basic dashi (see page 265)
15g (½ oz) light soy sauce
15g (½ oz) mirin
salt

For the soy-mirin sauce
30g (2 tbsp) soy sauce
30g (2 tbsp) mirin
5g (1 tsp) sugar

1 Use a sharp knife to split the anago open along the spine, and remove the innards and bones. Set the bones aside for later.

2 Heat a griddle pan over high heat and grill the anago until browned. Keep an eye on it as it can burn easily. Remove and slice into thick pieces.

3 Bring the dashi to the boil in a saucepan over high heat. Add the reserved anago bones and simmer for around 10 minutes, skimming away any scum that rises to the surface.

4 Rinse the rice well in cold water and drain. Put in a saucepan (or rice cooker) along with the dashi, and season with soy sauce, mirin and salt. Bring to the boil, reduce the heat to low and cook for 20–25 minutes, until the rice is tender.

5 Make the sauce by combining the soy sauce, mirin and sugar in a small saucepan. Bring to the boil and simmer over gentle heat for 2 minutes, until sticky.

6 Serve the rice divided into bowls. Arrange the slices of anago on top neatly and brush with the sticky sauce.

KAMATAMA UDON
Egg udon

Said to originate after a Yamago Udon customer recounted the joy of raw egg and soy sauce on his hot noodles, kamatama udon is a slippery kind of wonderful.

Kagawa, in the nort-east of Shikoku Island is known as the 'udon prefecture', being home to the highest concentration of udon noodle restaurants in Japan. The udon here is called 'sanuki udon' and is particularly firm and chewy.

Because of the unique texture and taste of sanuki udon, it has to be cooked simply. One such dish is *kamatama*, a Japanese-style carbonara. Raw egg envelops freshly boiled udon, a dash of soy sauce is added and the noodles slurped up immediately. The combination of runny egg and soy sauce is divine. Yamago Udon restaurant is said to be the birthplace of this humble dish.

Shinichi Yamakoshi, owner of Yamago Udon, makes his noodles by hand every day. 'Freshly made, firm sanuki udon are boiled. Rather than allowing them to drain and cool in cold water, as per usual methods, the noodles are dished straight from the pot, or the *kama*. This is where the name *kamatama* comes from. The noodles absorb water while boiling, and so I hope that you can enjoy the hot, chewy texture.'

At Yamago Udon, after first ordering the udon noodles, you select your side dish from various kinds of tempura lined up on the counter. This includes mainly vegetable tempura such as *gobo* (burdock) or *renkon* (lotus root), as well as *toriten*, a chicken tempura particular to this region. Each restaurant has their own distinct style so it's difficult to get tired of the noodles.

'As we would like you to enjoy several different restaurants, you can order from just one bowl of 200g of noodles,' suggests Shinichi. 'Some people do eat four to five bowls though!'

Chef //
Shinichi Yamakoshi
Location //
Yamago Udon, Kagawa

KAMATAMA UDON
Egg udon

Serves 2

Preparation time: 5 mins
Cooking time: 10 mins

400g (14 oz) udon noodles
2 eggs
2 tsp light soy sauce
1 spring onion, finely sliced

1 Bring a large pan of water to the boil and add the noodles. Cook according to the packet instructions until al dente.

2 Meanwhile, boil the kettle and pour hot water into the serving bowls to warm them.

3 Drain the noodles and immediately divide between the warmed bowls. Break an egg into each bowl and use chopsticks to mix vigorously. Sprinkle over the soy sauce and spring onion, and enjoy while hot.

TORINABE
Chicken and vegetable hotpot

Chicken soup from the soul of the prefecture's grey mountain village, the torinabe at Yamaai farm stay eases any hard-working heart.

Kamikatsu, small and hidden in the mountains, is known as the 'Leaf Business Village'. Its elderly residents became famous in Japan for building a multimillion-yen industry selling the foraged leaves, flowers and mountain vegetables used as decoration in traditional Japanese cuisine, known as *tsuma*.

A new business has now begun in Kamikatsu – farm stays. Following the success of the leaf business, many young people have moved to the village, or come to stay seasonally. The aim is for these people to stay in local homes as if they are with relatives, and experience the seasonal agricultural work of the village. This initiative was launched by the village as a whole, and is now highly popular with young people from urban areas. Yamaai is one such farm stay, which raises chickens famous as the brand Awaodori, a pride of Tokushima Prefecture. The *torinabe*, or chicken hotpot, they serve is hugely popular.

Owner Satoe Kishi says, 'We stew seasonal treats from the mountains in a chicken soup. In autumn, mushrooms picked in the mountains, and in winter, root vegetables such as daikon or turnip. In winter temperatures drop below zero, and so coming together around the fireplace and eating the *nabe* together is the greatest hospitality.'

The chicken soup, using consommé, is a deep, golden colour. It's delicious on its own, but when vegetables are added and stewed together, their *umami* flavours and scents melt through the soup. Then rice is added to the remaining soup, making a *zosui* or risotto, and finally, a freshly laid egg is mixed in.

'This rice was grown through natural methods in the terraced rice fields. The chicken's collagen is absorbed into each and every grain of rice, and even people who think they are already full always come back for seconds. Kamikatsu can be cut off through wind and snow in the winter, and so chicken is an important source of protein.' For visitors, this chicken hotpot is an addictive treat after working harder in the fields than they are probably used to.

Chef //
Satoe Kishi
Location //
Yamaai farm stay,
Kamikatsu

TORINABE
Chicken and vegetable hotpot

Serves 4

Preparation time: 10 mins
Cooking time: 2 hrs

500g (1lb) chicken pieces, cut into
  bite-sized pieces
1 tbsp soy sauce
2 tsp mirin
300g (10½ oz) Chinese cabbage, sliced into
  3–4cm (1¼–1½ in) square pieces
100g (3½ oz) daikon (white radish), cut into
  bite-sized pieces
50g (1¾ oz) spring onion (scallion), chopped
8 shiitak mushrooms, halved
1 block (200g/7 oz) firm tofu, cut into
  bite-sized pieces
200g (7 oz) cooked white rice (see page 264)
1 egg, beaten
salt

1 Fill a large stockpot with 2 litres (3½ pints) water and bring to the boil. Add the chicken pieces and simmer, partially covered, for 1–1½ hours, skimming away any scum that rises to the surface.

2 Add the soy sauce, mirin and the vegetables to the broth along with a pinch or two of salt. Simmer for 5–10 minutes, until the vegetables are just cooked. Add the tofu. Divide the chicken, vegetables and tofu between warmed serving bowls.

3 Stir the cooked rice into the broth and allow to heat through for a few minutes. Season to taste, stir through the beaten egg and immediately replace with the lid for 30 seconds. Ladle the rice and broth into the bowls and eat while piping hot.

NARUTO TAI NO SAKAMUSHI
Sake-steamed sea bream

If you asked the people the eastern part of Japan what their most beloved fish is the answer might be tuna – but those from Kansai would undoubtedly say tai (sea bream). The bright red bream is valued as a festive fish in Japan, and is a vital component of celebratory meals.

Sea bream is sourced from many of Japan's shores, but those from the Naruto straits connecting the islands of Honshu and Shikoku fetch the highest prices. The sea bream here is grown in the tides of the fast current of this area, giving it thick and tight flesh, with the pomp and dignity appropriate for the 'king of fish.'

There are several restaurants serving sea bream in Tokushima Prefecture. Hamagiku is one of those, and it is particularly renowned for its *sakamushi*, or sake-steamed dish. Here, the *kabuto* or head of the bream is steamed with sake and konbu seaweed. Head chef Toshihiro Hamada proudly claims that the Naruto sea bream is the best in Japan.

'The sea bream itself is the best of all Japan, and so we don't add too much flavor to the fish. We slice it from the gills, and remove the *kabuto*, steaming this generously. The deliciousness of the sea bream can be enjoyed as sashimi, but it is the gelatinous area around the bones which is the true delight of the bream. Even if it might seem rather bad manners, the best way to enjoy it is to slurp on the fish, bones and all.'

The sakamushi when delivered is a beautiful sight. As if demonstrating the freshness, the pectoral fin is taut. The sea bream is a fierce fish, which eats mostly squilla, shrimps and sometimes shellfish which live in the sand.

'First, eat the check flesh of the bream. This is the muscle it moves when hunting for prey, and it has a springy texture. Next, flip it over and take the part to which the gill is attached, and try slurping on it bones and all. You can enjoy the rich *umami* flavours that cling around the bone. And finally, the gelatin part of the fish's eye. People that really love bream will often fight over this eye.'

In the Kansai region, it is said that the restaurant is judged on what bream it has. Because this is a wild fish, it is not easy to catch. Owners go to the market first thing each morning to try to obtain good bream before it is taken by another restaurant.

'People who say that they don't like fish have not tried really delicious fish. It is said that Japanese cuisine is based on subtraction, and this means respecting the flavours of the ingredients themselves, and not adding any superfluous, unnecessary flavours. I think that this shows the highest respect towards the ingredients.'

Chef //
Toshihiro Hamada
Location //
Hamagiku, Tokushima
Prefecture

NARUTO TAI NO SAKAMUSHI
Sake-steamed sea bream

Serves 4

Preparation time: 15 minutes
Cooking time: 20 minutes

500–800g (1-1¾ lb) fresh sea bream,
  chopped into bite-sized pieces
15cm (6in) long kobu
300 ml (½ pint) sake
5–10g (1–2 tsp) light soy sauce
5g (1tsp) zest of yuzu (Japanese citrus),
  to serve

1 Place the kobu in a large heat-resistant dish and lie the sea bream on top.

2 Pour the sake over the sea bream. Place the dish in a steamer, cover and cook for 10–15 minutes.

3 Remove the lid and mix the soy sauce into the soup.

4 Serve topped with a sprinkling of yuzu zest.

FUKUMEN
Fukumen-style noodles

The name 'fukumen' translates as 'mask', but these noodles from Uwajima are first and foremost to be savoured with one's eyes.

The road runs along the sawtooth coastline of the cape, rising up and then falling at every corner. Eventually, a little dizzy, you arrive in Uwajima, a city situated on the western edge of Shikoku. Uwajima is among the most prominent fishing communities in Shikoku, its port crammed with fishing boats boasting a rich haul of *tai* (sea bream) and *aji* (horse mackerel). The fish here is sent to Tokyo's Tsukiji Fish Market where it demands high prices.

Uwajima is also home to a somewhat peculiar cuisine known as *fukumen*. Proprietor Seiji Iwata of Gansui, a long-established restaurant specialising in local Uwajima fare, stresses the importance of appearance when it comes to fukumen cuisine. It must be fit for the weddings and celebrations where it is most often served.

This dish uses gluten-free konnyaku noodles, made from the starch of a tuber called konjac or devil's tongue. Piled on top, the chef lavishly arranges the local specialties: red and white bream and *mikan* (mandarin orange) zest. The contrast of colours is striking. Although somewhat simple in taste, it is a dish for the health-conscious as it contains almost no carbohydrates, very few calories and just the right amount of protein.

Seiji says, 'Before eating, everything is stirred together thoroughly. This beautiful melange of colours, after stirring, transforms into a brown, sombre plate. Some families insist that the correct way to eat it is to stir clockwise from around the middle, retaining the visual spectacle for as long as possible'.

The practice of completely mixing together this perfectly assembled plate before eating is fitting for a country that adheres to the Buddhist principle of 'the impermanence of all things'. While ornate in appearance, the ingredients used are decidedly modest. According to the senior habitants of Uwajima, fukumen was originally devised by the locals many years ago in an age when fishing villages were poor, without much to eat, as a way of bringing a sense of celebration to their modest dinner tables. The traditions and morality of that impoverished age still reverberate in fukumen cuisine today.

Chef //
Seiji Iwata
Location //
Gansui, Uwajima and
Matsushima

FUKUMEN
Fukumen-style noodles

Serves 4

Preparation time: 5 mins
Cooking time: 20 mins

400g (14 oz) konyaku (shirataki) noodles
1 tbsp soy sauce
2 tsp mirin
1 tsp sugar, plus extra to season
100ml (3½ fl oz) basic dashi (see page 265)
200g (7 oz) white fish such as sea bass, bream
* or red mullet fillets*
½ tsp red food colouring
zest of 1 mandarin orange, finely chopped
4 spring onions (scallions), finely chopped
salt

1 Bring a pan of water to the boil and add the noodles. Cook for 10 minutes, skimming away the foam that rises to the surface. Drain.

2 Add the soy sauce, mirin, sugar and dashi to the pan and bring to a simmer. Return the noodles to the pan, bring back up to the boil and cook until the noodles have absorbed most of the dashi.

3 Meanwhile, bring water to boil in a pan and boil the fish for 3–5 minutes to get rid of any excess fats and oils. Transfer the fish to a hotpot, and then heat so that it loosens and crumbles. Season to taste with salt and sugar. When the fish has lost most of its moisture, transfer half the amount to a bowl and stir through the red food colouring.

4 Place the noodles on a large serving plate and carefully adorn with the fish, finely chopped mandarin and spring onions. Mix together well just before eating.

KAMABOKO
Cured fish cake

Before freezing technologies were available, fishermen faced the problem of how to preserve the fish from a massive catch. One solution came in the form of the fish paste kamaboko.

K amaboko is an essential ingredient for Japanese New Year cuisine. A seasoned fish paste, it's made by combining ground white fish flesh with egg whites, seasoning with salt and mirin, and then applying heat to firm it up. In the old days it would all go in a strip of bamboo and be heated over coals. And those days really are old, given the fact that kamaboko comes up in the *Tale of Genji*, Japan's oldest story, it has probably adorned dinner tables for over 1000 years.

Located in Kan'onji City in Kagawa Prefecture, Fukuya has always sourced the small fish for its kamaboko from the Inland Sea, renowned as one of the most nutrient-rich bodies of water in Japan. Right in the middle of its coast, Kan'onji City sits on the doorstep of a much-coveted fishing ground. Fukuya proprietor Kazuko Fukushima gives some background: 'You can catch all sorts of high-quality white flesh fish in the Inland Sea, including whiting, grunt, white croaker, and daggertooth pike conger. It is a veritable treasure chest for raw materials, and thanks to the regular distribution to Osaka and Kyoto, many kamaboko specialist shops took root here.'

As well as kamaboko made with white fish, Fukuya also make a version unique to the region using small shrimp called ebijako. After painstakingly removing their heads one by one, the shrimp are combined with white fish mince and tofu, and then fried in oil.

Kazuko is obsessed with the shrimp: 'Ebijako are delicious whether boiled, dried or used as an ingredient in other dishes. Their sweet meat can also be used to make a velvety stock. Frying them in oil gives off a mouthwatering fragrance to whet the appetite.'

While tasty on its own, kamaboko is also a perfect accompaniment to Japanese sake if eaten with freshly ground wasabi. This is called 'ita-wasa' in Japan, and abounds at New Year when Fukuya is at its busiest. Japanese New Year 'o-sechi' food simply must contain kamaboko, given its red and white colours that are auspicious for Japanese people.

Chef //
Kazuko Fukushima
Location //
Fukuya, Kan'onji
City, Kagawa

KAMABOKO
Cured fish cake

Serves 4

Cooking time: 40 mins

500g (1 lb 2 oz) skinless white fish
  fillet (such as sea bass, bream or cod),
  cut into chunks
2 egg whites
1 tbsp mirin
2 tsp sugar
1 tsp salt

You will need:
15cm (6in) x 5cm (2 in) strip of wood

1 Put the fish in a food processor and blitz to form a rough paste. Add egg whites, mirin, sugar and salt, and blitz again until very fine.

2 Using a fish slice, take some of the fish paste, coat the wooden strip, shaping it into a dome (semi-cylindrical) shape . Ensure that the surface is nice and smooth.

3 Place into a steamer and steam for about 10 minutes, until the fish is springy to the touch.

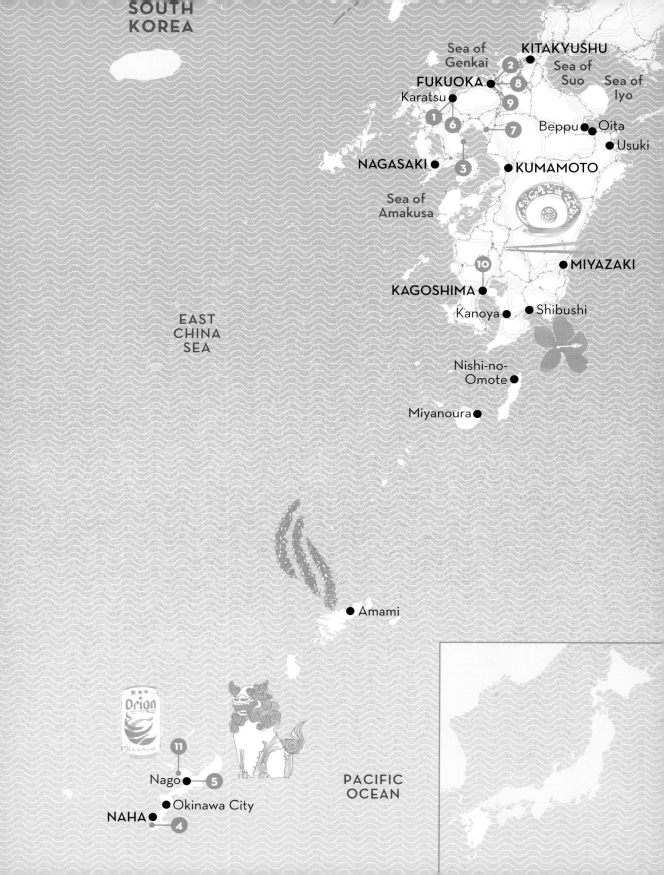

SOUTH
KOREA

Sea of
Genkai

KITAKYUSHU

2

Sea of
Suo

Sea of
Iyo

FUKUOKA

8

Karatsu

9

1

6

7

Beppu

Oita

Usuki

NAGASAKI

3

KUMAMOTO

Sea of
Amakusa

EAST
CHINA
SEA

10

MIYAZAKI

KAGOSHIMA

Kanoya

Shibushi

Nishi-no-
Omote

Miyanoura

Amami

Orion

11

Nago

5

PACIFIC
OCEAN

Okinawa City

NAHA

4

SOUTHERN JAPAN

With their subtropical climate, Okinawa and the southwest islands are known for pork dishes and a local cuisine notably distinct from that of other parts of Japan

WATEISHOKU
Ryokan tofu breakfast

One of Japan's most-beloved dishes is the traditional breakfast provided at a ryokan (Japanese-style inn). You may come across it in the more traditional home too, but most Japanese people these days have a Western-style breakfast, comprising bread and coffee.

Japanese traditional breakfasts can be summarised by the phrase *ichiju-sansai*, or 'one soup and three vegetables', referring to the one soup (miso) as a base, and three vegetables (or in fact three side dishes), eaten together with white rice, the staple food of Japan. There are certain rules to these three side dishes – vegetables must be seasonal, and while fish is permitted meat is not.

Kawashima Tofu, in the town of Karatsu by the Genkai Sea, has been specializing in making tofu for over 300 years. The breakfast served here is naturally centred around tofu, accompanied by a thick omelette and dried fish. Tofu is now eaten all over the world, yet the delicious taste of the variety made from domestic soy beans with high quality local spring water is on a special level. The zaru tofu, named after the *zaru* (colander) through which the basic oboro tofu is strained, is full of rich soy flavour, making you keen for seconds before you have finished your first bite.

According to the owner of Kawashima Tofu, Kawashima Yoshimasa, 'Because we are a tofu shop, we use tofu as the main ingredient in our breakfast, together with local Karatsu rice, vegetables and fish. As the first meal of the day, we consider nutritional balance, to make a taste that you cannot get tired of.'

Until 50 years ago, the ichiju-sansai style of meal was embedded in every home. However, along with the inflow of Western culture, the eating habits of Japanese people have become Westernised. But somehow the ichiju-sansai DNA is still in the blood. Whenever they return from long trips overseas, the first food almost all Japanese people seek out is a traditional breakfast.

Chef //
Kawashima Yoshimasa
Location //
Kawashima Tofu, Karatsu

WATEISHOKU
Ryokan tofu breakfast

Serves 4

Preparation time: 5 mins
Cooking time: 30 mins

2 mackerel fillets (about 150g/5½ oz total)
300g (10½ oz) rice, cooked according to page 264
salt

For the miso soup
340g (12 oz) silken tofu
40g (1½ oz) spring onions (scallions), finely sliced
300ml (10 fl oz) basic dashi (see page 265)
30g (1 oz) miso

For the omelette
3 eggs
1 tbsp mirin
½ tsp sugar
1 tsp soy sauce
cooking oil, for frying

1 Make the omelette. In a bowl, beat together the eggs, mirin, sugar and soy sauce. Heat the oil in a tamago-yakiki (a rectangular pan for making Japanese omelettes), or non-stick frying pan, over medium-high heat. When hot, add a ladleful of the egg mixture to the pan, just enough to make a thin, even layer. Wait a few seconds for the egg to begin to set, then use a pair of chopsticks to roll the omelette into a log towards the other end of the pan. Add a bit more oil, then add another ladleful of the egg mixture, tilting the pan to coat. Wait a few seconds and then roll the log back to the other end of the pan, gathering the new layer of egg as you go. Repeat until done.

2 Remove the omelette from the pan and put on a chopping board. Trim the ends off and then slice into thin ribbons. Set aside.

3 Drain the tofu and press between paper towels to extract excess moisture. Cut it into four pieces. Set aside while you cook the fish.

4 Season the fish fillets with salt. Preheat your grill and cook the fish for 2–3 minutes on each side, until golden and just cooked.

5 Bring the dashi to the boil in a saucepan. Add the miso, tofu and spring onions and stir gently to dissolve the miso and heat the tofu through. Taste and add more miso, if necessary.

6 Divide the cooked rice, miso soup, omelette and grilled fish into separate bowls and serve.

TONKOTSU RAMEN

While perhaps originally from China, ramen has undergone its own evolution in Japan, where it is beloved by all. Ippudo Daimyo Honten, the most famous tonkotsu-style ramen joint in Kitakyushi, has a distinctive milky-white pork bone broth.

With over 10,000 ramen shops throughout the country, each region prides itself on its own individual taste and style. Ramen's popularity has spread overseas, and enthusiasts travel from all around the world to learn from Japan's master ramen chefs. Kitakyushu, in the Fukuoka Prefecture, boasts the particular style known as tonkotsu ramen. The broth is made from pork bones – the 'tonkotsu' of the name. The bones simmer away in a large pan for hours on end, the chef occasionally skimming the surface to achieve the characteristic milky white broth. It looks extremely rich but is surprisingly light.

The noodles of authentic Kyushu ramen are cooked so that the centre still remains hard. When ordering ramen, you can choose how hard or soft you like your noodles – using the distinctive words of *barigane* (very hard), *barikata* (al dente), *futsu* (normal) and *yawamen* (soft) to express your preferred style. There is also a system called *kaedama*, in which you can order a refill of noodles to enjoy with the remaining soup.

Tonkotsu ramen was first created as a quick and cheap fast food for people working in heavy labour at the fish market. It was the Fukuoka ramen shop Ippudo that transformed this humble food into a new representative Japanese cuisine to rival sushi and tempura. Ippudo remains the most famous tonkotsu ramen shop in the country.

More than anything, the taste of Ippudo's soup is delicious. And for good reason. The soup is cooked for 18 hours and then left for a whole day at a low temperature before a soy-based broth called *kaeshi* is stirred through. The wheat noodles are carefully selected and prepared with a little water. Their crisp yet slippery texture matches the soup perfectly. The final piece of the puzzle is the *char siu* barbecued pork used as a topping. It's made from simmering both pork shoulder and belly meat.

Manager of the Ippudo Daimyo Honten Saito Junya says of his ramen-making philosophy, 'I always ask myself how I can make today's dish better than yesterday's. How can I come up with a quality of flavour that will be enjoyed by all our customers?'

Chef //
Saito Junya (manager)
Location //
Ippudo Daimyo Honten,
Fukuoka

TONKOTSU RAMEN

Serves 4

Preparation time: 30 mins
Cooking time: at least 18 hours

For the tonkotsu (pork bone) broth
1kg (2 lb 3 oz) pork leg bones
3l (5 pints) water
50g (1¾ oz) spring onions (scallions), finely
  chopped, to garnish
2 eggs, hard boiled, to serve

For the char siu sauce
30ml (1 fl oz) soy sauce
30ml (1 fl oz) Chinese rice wine
60ml (1¼ fl oz) water
150g (5½ oz) pork belly
750g (1 lb 11 oz) fresh Chinese-style ramen
  noodles (if fresh noodles aren't available,
  use dried)
salt, to taste

1 Start by making the broth. Place the pork bones in a large stockpot and fill with plenty of water. Bring to a rapid boil over high heat, drain and rinse thoroughly to remove any remaining blood. This step will result in a clearer, more refined broth.

2 Place the rinsed bones in a clean stockpot, add the water and bring to a boil. Cook uncovered over medium-low heat for 18 hours, skimming any foam that rises to the surface and stirring occasionally. Expect the stock to boil down considerably, so top up with fresh water as necessary – the broth should be milky white in colour.

3 In a saucepan, add the soy sauce, rice wine and water, followed by the pork belly. Bring to the boil over high heat. Reduce the heat to low and simmer to reduce for about 1½ hours to create the char siu sauce.

4 Remove the pork from the pan and thinly slice. Set aside.

5 Bring a large pan of water to the boil and cook the noodles for 2 minutes, or until just tender but still firm to bite. (Alternatively, cook according to the packet instructions.) Drain and divide between serving bowls.

6 Add a teaspoon of the char siu sauce and a pinch of salt to each bowl with the noodles. Ladle the hot broth over the top and garnish with spring onions, half an egg per bowl, and slices of the char siu pork.

GANEMESHI
Crab rice

Crab rice shouldn't be eaten in a polite or dainty way – instead, enjoy huge bites. The scent of the ocean which bursts through your mouth is irresistible.

The sea that has been in front of you for half the day suddenly disappears, revealing vast tidal flats that extend for several kilometres off the coast. The Ariake Sea is said to have the world's largest tidal variation of 8 metres, and is known as 'the sea that shows the pull of the moon'.

The sea is also famous for its swimmer crabs, or *gane*, known to be the finest tasting crabs of all Japan, likely because of the rich nutrients of the sea. During the day, the sun bakes the exposed flats, which are then swept away again by the reversing tide. The tiny organisms that proliferated in the sun now drift through the sea to finally settle and accumulate. Since the dawn of the Japanese archipelago, the force of the moon has been nourishing this fertile sea.

'The flats are the cradle of life. The treasures from this sea have a rich taste, and are said to grow faster than in any other. Thanks to the flow coming in from the large rivers, it is also rich in nutrients,' says Hisago chef Rikio Kawashima proudly.

The fishermen set a net at a depth of 10 metres, trapping the crabs as they swim by, deftly using their oar-shaped legs. In summer, the fatty male crabs are highly prized, while from autumn to winter, the fine flavour of the female egg-bearing crabs is preferred.

In Takezaki Town, where Rikio lives, there are around 20 restaurants specialising in crab. Here, as well as elsewhere, the usual way to eat crab is boiled. A mix of sea and fresh water is used, salty just to the point of being drinkable.

The boiled crab meat is delicious as it is. However, local fishermen favour *ganemeshi*, or crab rice. The boiled crab meat is placed on top of freshly cooked rice, and soy sauce is poured over the top. The trick is to mix in a small amount of the cooking water from the crab with the flesh. The rich flavours are taken up by the rice. It's heavenly.

Chef //
Rikio Kawashima
Location //
Kappo Hisago, Takezaki

GANEMESHI
Crab rice

Serves 4–6

Preparation time: 30 mins
Cooking time: 10 mins plus cooking
   time for the rice

350–400g (12½–14 oz) whole crab
450g (1lb) rice, cooked according to page 264
1 tbsp soy sauce
sea salt

1 Bring a large pan of lightly salted water to the boil. Add the crab and cook for 10 minutes. Remove from the heat drain the crab, reserving about 1 tablespoon of the cooking liquid. Set the crab aside for 10 minutes.

2 When cool enough to handle, shell the crab. Remove the triangular abdomen flap, open its carapace and remove the dead man's fingers. (The base of the claws and the brain are considered the tastiest parts.) Put in a bowl and add the reserved cooking liquid and add a dash or two of soy sauce.

3 Place the crab on top of freshly cooked hot rice and eat it up.

IMAIYU BUTTER SAUTÉ

Crisp-fried fish with garlic and butter sauce

Even locals dismiss Okinawan fish as beautiful but bland. But with some old sea-wisdom Hiroyasu Tamaki of Itoman Gyomin Shokudo dishes up fish as fine as their colourful scales.

Itoman city on the southernmost tip of Okinawa is home to many fishermen, who for years, have rowed their plank-built canoes out through high waves into the open ocean to catch fish. Hiroyasu Tamaki, was born into a fish dealer household and spent his formative years by the sea of Itoman, learning the lore of the fishermen. He became inspired to start his own fish restaurant for an odd reason: 'I'd always been told that the colourful Okinawan fish that are red, blue and yellow are great to look at in an aquarium but taste no good at all. It is true that fish found in Okinawa's waters taste somewhat bland and plain. Having said that, if you can figure out the varieties of fish and the seasons, and how to season them, you get delicious local cuisine unique to the area.'

His specialty fish dish is imaiyu butter sauté. In Okinawan dialect, *imaiyu* means 'fresh', and they are. All the fish come straight from the nearby market. The most popular on the blackboard menu is a white fish called *gitaro*, which is twice-cooked, helping to bring out its fragrant flavour. Hiroyasu explains, 'Okinawa fish swim in warm waters, so their flesh is not all firmed up. The first round of frying seals in the tastiness, and the second frying brings out the fragrance of the fish. The fish tastes light and fluffy, and melts in the mouth.' Once chosen and cooked, the fish is served with a buttery sauce with the addition of asa seaweed, unique to Okinawa, and garlic.

Hiroyasu continues: 'As well as tourists who come here on holiday, I want locals to rediscover the traditional food culture of Itoman, in fact of Okinawa as a whole. To do this, as well as carrying on old traditions, it is important to challenge the new as well. From the edge of Japan, I want to show the world how great Okinawa is.'

Chef //
Hiroyasu Tamaki
Location //
Itoman Gyomin
Shokudo, Naha

IMAIYU
BUTTER SAUTÉ
Crisp-fried fish with
garlic and butter sauce

Serves 4

Preparation time: 5 mins
Cooking time: 15 mins

400g (14oz) whole white fish such as sea
  bream or perch, cleaned and scaled
30g (1 oz) plain flour
20g (¾ oz) butter
2 cloves garlic, chopped
10g (½ oz) dried asa seaweed, or other kelp
salt and pepper

1 Pour enough oil to come up to 5cm (2in) in a wok or large frying pan, place over medium-high heat and bring up to 170°C/340°F (use a thermometer). The very hot oil should bubble vigorously when tested with a chopstick.

2 Season the fish with salt and pepper and dredge lightly in flour. Carefully slide into the hot oil and fry both sides for 5 minutes, until golden. Remove and drain on kitchen paper.

3 Heat the butter in a clean frying pan until frothy. Add the fish and spoon the butter over the fish, frying for a couple of minutes. Remove the fish from the butter using a slotted spoon, and place on a serving plate.

4 Next, add the garlic and dried asa to the butter in the pan, then season to taste. Take off the heat and pour the hot buttery sauce all over the fried fish and serve immediately.

SOKI SOBA
Okinawan pork rib ramen with a pork broth

Soki soba is the iconic dish of Okinawa, famous for its love of pork. At Brazil Shokudo, chef Akio Yamashita rounds off this local favourite with a South American espresso.

South American food has found its way on to the menus in Okinawa, thanks in part to locals who emigrated to Brazil and Argentina and then returned. Brazil Shokudo in Nago City, in the northern part of Okinawa, is no exception. Take a closer look at the Brazilian flag hanging outside and you'll see a *suba* in the middle, the bowl used for Okinawan ramen.

As well as noodles, the menu also includes chicken roasted South American style and also *feijoada*, a stew of beans with beef and pork that is true Brazilian soul food. The high point of the meal for some is the espresso, made with South American beans. Owner Akio Yamashita, as well as being dedicated to the flavours of South America learned from his returned émigré parents, is also obsessed with *soki soba*, a much-loved dish in Okinawan households: 'While Okinawa's suba looks a lot like ramen, which has its roots in China, in fact that method of making the soup with dried bonito and pork bones is unique to Okinawa. With these noodles, we serve *soki* (stewed pork ribs), which have been cooked with a salty-sweet soy sauce'.

Akio believes that a concept called *chanpuru* (meaning 'mixed') is at the core of Okinawan cuisine: 'From long ago Okinawa had connections with China, Taiwan and other Asian countries, and then after the war the occupation forces built bases here. And of course, Japanese mainland culture is a major influence. I believe that these flavours from all sorts of lands created a taste only found in Okinawa.'

In Okinawa, despite the perpetual summer, people enjoy soki soba piping hot. A few slurps in and sweat starts to gush, but the deep-bodied soup made with fatty pork is simply irresistible. Midway through, you add a few drops of a flavouring made with the local firewater Awamori and chilli peppers, and the taste changes dramatically.

As soon as I put down my chopsticks, Yamashita brings over an espresso. Soba noodles and espresso, a truly distinctive meld of Okinawa and South America.

Chef //
Akio Yamashita
Location //
Brazil Shokudo, Nago

SOKI SOBA

Okinawan pork rib ramen with a pork broth

Serves 4

Cooking time: 4 hrs

800 g (1lb 12oz) pork loin ribs, trimmed
   of cartilage
2 tbsp soy sauce
2 tbsp sake
2 tsp mirin
1 tbsp sugar
400g (14oz) basic dashi (see page 265)
320g (11oz) Okinawa soba, or Chinese egg
   noodles
1 spring onion (scallion), finely chopped
salt and pepper
5g (¼ oz) pickled ginger

1. Cover the ribs in cold water and bring to the boil to leach out their blood. Discard the water and rinse the ribs, then place them back in the pan.

2. Pour in 600ml (20½ fl oz) fresh water and bring to the boil. Simmer over medium heat for 2–3 hours, until the ribs are quite soft, and skimming away any foam that rises to the surface. Strain and set aside both the ribs and the broth.

3. In a saucepan, combine the pork ribs, soy sauce, sake, mirin and sugar, and cook for 1 hour.

4. Combine the pork broth with the katsuo dashi and bring to a gentle boil. Season with salt and pepper, and keep warm.

5. Bring a pan of water to the boil and cook the noodles according to the packet instructions.

6. To serve, divide the noodles between bowls, pour over the hot broth, add the ribs and garnish with finely chopped spring onion and pickled ginger.

ARADAKI
Soy-simmered fish

In a land surrounded by ocean, the most popular dish to complement rice is aradaki, fish simmered with sake, sugar, soy sauce and mirin.

There is a saying in Japan: 'There are no manners for aradaki.' You can be delicate with your chopsticks eating the flesh of the fish of course, which *is* tasty. But in aradaki the gelatinous area around the bones is particularly prized and at its pinnacle in the fish head, known in Japanese as the *kabuto*, which is much-favoured and often fought over. The head is difficult to eat with chopsticks, so it's best to take it in your hands and slurp it up.

Yoyokaku is a traditional Japanese restaurant in Karatsu on the Genkai Sea, renowned in Kyushu. Aradaki is generally a meal to be eaten at home, but the one at Yoyokaku is a feast. Their truly delicious aradaki has a clear, pure taste. The flesh is full, and comes easily off the bone. Each part of the fish comes with a different taste and umami. And of course, it goes superbly with rice and alcohol.

In Japan, while it is said that people who eat aradaki in an attractive way will themselves be attractive, you can distinguish someone who really enjoys good food by how thoroughly they eat this dish. And a chef will never forget a customer who cleanly devours the whole fish, leaving only the bones. They are guaranteed to be served the freshest ingredients of the day the next time they visit the restaurant.

Chef //
Masayasu Okouchi
Location //
Yoyokaku, Karatsu

ARADAKI
Soy-simmered fish

Serves 4

Preparation time: 10 mins
Cooking time: 15 mins

500g (1 lb 2 oz) white-fleshed fish (sea bream or
*   sea bass) fillets, cut into chunks*
500ml (17 fl oz) water
200ml (7 fl oz) sake
1 burdock root (about 100g/3½ oz), thinly sliced
30g (1 oz) ginger, thinly sliced
70–90ml (2¼–3 fl oz) soy sauce
60g (2 oz) sugar
100ml (3½ fl oz) mirin
steamed vegetables, to serve

1 Bring a pan of water to the boil. Add the fish and bring the water back up to the boil. Cook for just a few seconds, then remove immediately with a slotted spoon into a bowl of iced water.

2 Place the water and sake over high heat and bring to the boil, add the burdock and ginger, then add the fish. Keeping the heat high, simmer for 10–15 mins or until the liquid has reduced by about one-third.

3 Stir in the sugar, mirin and soy sauce, then continue to simmer for a couple more minutes. Tilt the pan on an angle and spoon over the seasoned liquid over the fish until the liquid has almost completely evaporated.

4 Arrange the fish on a serving dish and garnish with steamed, seasonal vegetables.

UNAGI NO SEIRO MUSHI
Steamed eel and seasoned rice

At Ganso Motoyoshiya, sweet and salty rice is steamed with grilled eel on top, its fragrant umami infusing the rice. A sauce that is literally 300 years old helps.

The city of Yanagawa in the northern part of Kyushu Island has the most eel eateries of all Japan. With a population of 70,000 people, the city features around 70 eel specialty restaurants. Fresh wild eel could once be caught in the river that runs through the town, amid the brackish waters where fresh and seawater meet. However, the majority of eel on the market today is farmed. While wild eel is certainly delicious, the taste varies greatly according to the location, season and feed. Farmed eel has the twin benefits of being of good quality throughout the year and very tasty.

Eel is usually prepared in a style called *kabayaki*, where a live eel is gutted and strung onto a skewer and char-grilled. However, in Yanagawa, eel is first prepared in the kabayaki way then placed on rice flavoured with a sweet and salty sauce, and steamed. A wooden box known as a *seiro* is used for the steaming, leading to the name *seiro mushi*.

Ganso Motoyoshiya is a restaurant that has specialised in the seiro mushi style since the Edo period. The key is the sauce, which has been passed on and replenished over the 300-year period since the restaurant's foundation. Having been grilled on a super-hot coal, the eel is plunged into this sauce, with which the rich fat of the eel mixes. Over 100 eels are grilled here daily, meaning that the extract of these 100-odd eels is added to the sauce. And over the 300-year history of the restaurant, the extract of countless eels has now infused its way in. This sauce then is both the tradition and the treasure of the restaurant. It's unique and very special.

However, it is possible that soon we won't be able to eat the eel in question. The juvenile eel, necessary for eel farming, is drastically reduced in the wild. Until complete farming of the eel becomes possible, a meal enjoyed by common people in the Edo period will remain an expensive delicacy.

Chef //
Tsutomu Motoyoshi
Location //
Ganso Motoyoshiya,
Yanagawa

UNAGI NO SEIRO MUSHI

Steamed eel and seasoned rice

Serves 4

Preparation time: 30 mins
Cooking time: 15 mins

200g (7 oz) freshly cooked rice (see page 264)
100g (3½oz) eel, filleted
1 egg
pinch each of sugar and salt
dash of cooking oil, for frying

For the sauce
200ml (7 fl oz) soy sauce
200ml (7 fl oz) mirin
100ml (3½ fl oz) sugar

1 Combine the sauce ingredients in a small saucepan and simmer over a medium heat for 3 minutes.

2 Grill the eel fillets over charcoal skin-side down first, turning occasionally, for about 10 to 15 minutes or until they are golden brown. Brush the sauce over them, then grill again for a few minutes.

3 Put the rice into a heatproof bowl. Pour the sauce over the rice and arrange the chargrilled eel on top.

4 Beat the egg in a bowl and add a pinch of sugar and salt. Heat the oil in a frying pan and pour in the egg. Tilt the pan to spread the egg into a thin layer and cook for 1 minute. Flip over and cook the other side until done. Remove from the pan and slice into thin strips.

5 Scatter the egg strips over the eel and rice. Steam for around 10 minutes and serve.

'An eel artisan takes three years to learn to gut, and a lifetime to grill. My mission is passing on our traditional method of cooking, which has continued for 300 years, to the next generation exactly as it is.'

Tsutomu Motoyoshi, president of Ganso Motoyoshiya

YAKITORI
Grilled meat

Take a 15cm (6 in) bamboo skewer, put meat on it, grill it on charcoals and eat it with sauce. You have discovered paradise, or as the Japanese term it, yakitori.

In Kyushu, *yakitori* is almost always made with pork, and specifically pork belly – but it can be made with chicken or beef instead, or even seafood such as octopus. More than anything, it's cheap – around 100 yen (60p/$1) per stick. You slip some raw cabbage in between the meat sticks and dip it in a sweet and sour sauce. This is a meal enjoyed by labourers, together with beer.

The fun of yakitori is in the limitless variations. You can enjoy mixing ingredients, and sauces vary from traditional Japanese flavours to Western styles.

Akinori Yashima of the restaurant Hachi-Bei in Fukuoka is a leading chef, who takes this common person's yakitori and serves it as a cuisine comparable to tempura or sushi. One elevated skewer becomes a complete dish: take his chicken wings, splashed with *daiginjo* sake then grilled on 900°C coals. When you bite into them, the balance of the crispy skin and the meat, with piping hot juices, is irresistible. Simple is best.

The delectable skewer with meat, mini tomatoes, small green *shishito* peppers and octopus allows you to savour both the flavours of the ocean and the mountains at once. Each of the ingredients stands out with its distinctive texture and flavour – the juicy pork, slightly acidic tomatoes, bitter peppers and crunchy octopus.

The most popular of all the skewers is the sukiyaki kushi. Slightly bitter *shungiku*, or garland chrysanthemum, is wrapped with beef, and this is eaten dipped in a salty-sweet sauce with raw egg yolk. Your mouth fills with the flavours of sukiyaki.

Akinori says, 'Even overseas, if you just take some skewers you can make a full-course meal from whatever local foods there might be. The ideas are endless. It is fun to create hit menu items, which customers will always come back to. All it really is is putting ingredients onto a skewer and grilling them, yet, this really questions the flexibility of the cook's mind.'

Chef //
Akinori Yashima
Location //
Hachi-Bei, Fukuoka

YAKITORI
Grilled meat

Serves 4

Preparation time: 10 mins
Cooking time: 15 mins

100g (3½ oz) beef loin, thinly sliced
300g (10 oz) shungiku (garland
*   chrysanthemum) or watercress, chopped into*
*   4cm lengths*
sake, for brushing
4 egg yolks, beaten, to serve

For the sukiyaki sauce
100ml (3½ fl oz) soy sauce
50ml (1½ fl oz) mirin
50ml (1½ fl oz) sake
100ml (3½ fl oz) tsp sugar

You will need:
4 bamboo skewers, soaked in water

1 Lay a thinly sliced piece of beef flat on a surface. Place 50g of shungiku or watercress at one end, and roll them together towards the end of the beef slice. Wrap tightly to ensure that it is secure. Once ready, thread on to the bamboo skewers.

2 Preheat your barbecue and get the coals burning hot. Brush the skewers with sake and grill until browned, turning occasionally.

3 Meanwhile, place the ingredients for the sukiyaki sauce in a saucepan over a medium heat, stirring gently, until the alcohol has evaporated.

4 Once grilled, dip the skewers in the sukiyaki sauce and arrange on a serving plate. Serve with the egg yolk on the side for dipping.

MIZUTAKI
Chicken hotpot

Using only water and chicken, this hotpot is a famous traditional cure for Kyushu winters. In the icy winds blowing from the Sea of Japan nothing warms you more quickly.

Mizutaki dates from the Edo period. It falls somewhere between a Western consommé soup and a Chinese white broth. While its appearance is quite plain, the flavours of the chicken melt into the soup, creating a deep, rich taste.

No further ingredients need to be added to the soup at all, although in Fukuoka, it's eaten with the strong citrus kick of ponzu sauce. Another accent often used is *yuzu kosho*, a rich condiment made from the salt-preserved skin of the citrus fruit yuzu and green chillies.

As well as meat, adding vegetables such as cabbage brings a smooth sweetness into the soup, making it all the more delicious. Vegetables with high water content dilute the taste of the soup, so cabbage is preferred. Suffused in the chicken stock, it can seem possible to eat an endless amount of this cabbage.

Leftover mizutaki soup is enjoyed as *zosui*. Some people even eat mizutaki just for the purpose of this step. Cooked rice is added to the rich soup, with its concentrated chicken stock umami. After adding a pinch of salt, a beaten egg is poured over the mixture. Each individual grain of rice soaks up the umami of the chicken, and it is almost impossible to stop eating bowl upon bowl.

Hirokatsu Okutsu, head chef of mizutaki restaurant Toriden, was previously a chef of traditional Japanese cuisine. He says of the secret to delicious mizutaki, 'Firstly, spare no effort with the ingredients. The chicken should be freshly killed that morning. All of the scum should be thoroughly skimmed from the base soup, ensuring that the smell of the meat is fully removed. With such effort in the soup, we want it to be enjoyed right to the very last drop.'

Winter in Fukuoka is arctic. Icy seasonal winds make you hunch up in the cold, and eating mizutaki is perfect for warming you up from the inside.

Chef //
Hirokatsu Okutsu
Location //
Toriden, Fukuoka

MIZUTAKI
Chicken hotpot

Serves 4

Preparation time: 1 hr
Cooking time: 20 mins

½ head cabbage, cut into chunks
200g (7 oz) tofu, cubed
40g (1½ oz) rice (optional)
1 egg (optional)

For the broth
1 × 1.3kg (2 lb 14 oz) whole chicken
2 litres (68 fl oz) water

For the ponzu sauce
200ml (7 oz) yuzu or lemon juice
200ml (7 oz) soy sauce
100ml (3½ oz) mirin

1 Place the chicken into a large stockpot, pour over the water and bring to the boil over high heat. Simmer for around 3–4 hours, skimming off the scum from the surface. Top up with a little more water occasionally if needed.

2 Remove the chicken from the broth and set aside on a chopping board to cool enough to handle. Take the meat off the bones and cut it into bite-sized chunks.

3 Bring the broth back up to the boil, add the chicken followed by the cabbage and tofu. Simmer for 5 minutes, until the cabbage is just tender but still has some bite.

4 In a bowl, stir together the ponzu sauce ingredients.

5 When the hotpot is ready, serve with the ponzu sauce for dipping on the side.

6 Optional: Leftover broth can be brought back up to the boil, rice added and seasoned to taste. When the rice is cooked, pour in beaten egg. Place the lid on and turn off the heat to allow the egg to cook in the residual heat. Ladle into soup bowls to serve.

SHABU-SHABU

Swishing thin slices of pork through a konbu seaweed broth makes the sound 'shabu-shabu'. This onomatopoeic word has become the name of the dish

The origins of shabu-shabu are in China, where lamb is traditionally the base. Yet in Japan, it is almost exclusively pork, and specifically, thinly sliced belly meat, with a large amount of fat. Kurobuta pork from Kagoshima is a representative high-grade brand of this meat in Japan, exported to Europe and around the world. The fatty meat of this naturally raised swine becomes very sweet once placed on the heat. Because the fat has a low melting point, when placed in the pan it is ready to eat once the colour changes. Consequently, the trick to preparing shabu-shabu is not to allow the konbu broth to come to the boil, and to swirl the meat through at a temperature of around 80°C. If the broth boils, the meat will only become tough.

The supporting cast to bring out the flavours of shabu-shabu is *negi* (leek) and tofu. Wrapping the shabu-shabu meat around the negi and eating them together creates a particularly delightful, crunchy texture.

Actually, the shabu-shabu cooking method works well with other dishes and can be applied to meat, fish or any ingredients. For example, fish such as sea bream or amberjack can be thinly sliced and cooked shabu-shabu style in konbu broth, creating a sumptuous hotpot. The key, whether using meat or fish, is to slice thinly on a 45-degree angle. It should be at a thickness where it is possible to see through the meat, then this is 'shabu-shabu'ed for just a few seconds. If it is too thickly sliced it will not have a good texture, and the reason for using the method will be lost, so care should be taken at this stage.

To finish off, udon noodles are recommended. The concentrated umami flavours of the pork makes just the kind of luxury soup that slippery udon noodles love to drink.

Location //
Karen, 3-12
Yamanokuchichō,
Kagoshima

SHABU-SHABU

Serves 4

Preparation time: 10 mins
Cooking time: 10 mins

2 litres (68 fl oz) water
5cm (2 in) piece kombu
500g (1 lb 2oz) pork belly, thinly sliced
100g (3½ oz) tofu
200g (7 oz) Chinese cabbage,
  roughly chopped
50g (1½ oz) leeks, roughly
  chopped
udon noodles (optional)

For the sauce
100ml (3½ fl oz) soy sauce
300g (10½ oz) grated daikon (white radish),
  drained and squeezed of excess water

1 Bring the water to boil in a saucepan and add the kombu. Pour in a cupful of water, which will lower the heat slightly.

2 Add a few of the pork slices, and use chopsticks to shabu-shabu (swirl) it around in the simmering water. Remove once the pork has turned white. Next, add your tofu and vegetables and let them simmer for 1 minute. Finally, add the remaining pork and simmer until done. Place the pork and vegetables on a platter.

3 Combine the soy sauce and grated daikon in a bowl and serve alongside the pork and vegetables for dipping.

4 Optional: Once all the pork and vegetables have been enjoyed, add the udon to the remaining broth and bring to a simmer. Cook for around 3 minutes, and eat the udon dipped into soy-daikon dipping sauce.

IKASUMI-SHIRU
Squid ink soup

Okinawans prize the health-giving properties of food. Accordingly, squid ink soup is lauded for aiding digestion. That the katsuobushi (dried bonito flakes) and pork make a delicious broth is a bonus.

Squid ink is eaten in only certain parts of the world, and it is said that these are limited to Italy, Spain and Okinawa, but not elsewhere in Japan. It is highly rated for encouraging gastric progress and cleansing the gut. Traditionally, women of Okinawa would eat a soup made from thick squid ink as their first food after giving birth.

About an hour outside the central Okinawan city of Naha lies the town Motobu, deep within the green forest known as Yanbaru. Here, the restaurant Sashimitei is famous for its home-style cooking, centred on local Okinawan fish. Squid ink soup, or ikasumi-shiru, is a popular menu item.

'Unless the squid ink is fresh, it loses its richness and sheen, which are most important. If you eat this before going out your teeth will be dyed black and it is hard to remove, however it is said that the fresher the squid ink is the less it sticks to you.' So says manager of Sashimitei Zentaro Kakazu, laughing. For squid ink, white squid is used. Okinawa is one of the leading areas for squid in Japan, and squid specifically for ink is sold at the fresh fish markets.

'Squid ink helps to regulate the functions of the intestines,' says Zentaro, 'and it is effective when you have a hangover or are tired. It is eaten very often in Okinawan homes. You can also cook rice in the leftover soup to make *kurijushi*, which is really delicious.'

Zentaro, like all Okinawan people, always speaks about health when talking about food. This is connected to the value of taking care of one another. For centuries, Okinawa has received visitors by ship from all parts of the world. It is said that the culture of hospitality towards people who reached these islands after long journeys is at the core of Okinawan cuisine today. In fact, it is thought likely that cooking with squid ink was introduced to Okinawa by missionaries from Europe.

Chef //
Zentaro Kakazu
Location //
Sashimitei,
Motobu, Okinawa

IKASUMI-SHIRU
Squid ink soup

Serves 4

Preparation time: 10 mins
Cooking time: 15 mins

1.5 litres (51 fl oz) basic dashi (see
  page 265)
500g (1 lb 2 oz) squid, cleaned and
  cut into bite-sized pieces
200g (7 oz) pork belly, cut into
  bite-sized pieces
2 × 4g squid ink sachets
handful of greens or leeks, shredded
250g (9 oz) Okinawan island tofu, or tofu
soy sauce
salt
miso paste, to taste (optional)

1 Heat the stock in a large pan. Add the squid
and pork belly, and simmer over medium heat
for 5 minutes.

2 Add the greens or leeks and stir in the squid ink.

3 Season with soy sauce and salt to taste. You
could also add a spoonful of miso paste if you
like a stronger flavour.

BASIC RECIPES

KAMADAKI GOHAN
Kamado-cooked rice

A kamado is a traditional Japanese wood or charcoal stove. If you don't have a kamado, use the gohan recipe (right), which requires no specialist equipment.

This recipe comes from Soranone Shokudou, a restaurant on the shores of Lake Biwa.

Serves 2
Preparation time: 30 mins
Cooking time: 20 mins

Ingredients
300g (10½ oz) short-grain white rice

1 Wash the rice in a large bowl with a small amount of water, carefully rubbing each grain, and changing the water regularly until the water runs somewhat clear. This is known as to togu rice in Japanese.

2 Fill the bowl with fresh water and allow the rice to soak for 30 minutes.

3 Drain the rice and place in an earthen pot with 300ml (10 fl oz) water, and place on the fire. When it comes to boil and steams, reduce the heat to low and cook for 8–10 minutes. Remove from the heat once a crispy aroma comes out of the pot.

4 Steam the rice with the lid on for 10 minutes, or until the rice is tender, then remove the lid. Use a paddle (known as a shamoji) or a spatula to fold the rice gently, trying not to break the grains too much.to boil and steams, reduce the heat to low and cook for 8–10 minutes. Remove from the heat once a crispy aroma comes out of the pot.

GOHAN
Japanese steamed rice

Rice is Japan's primary culinary staple; the name *gohan* means, quite simply, 'meal' – and no meal is considered complete without it.

Gohan is always made with short-grain white rice.

Serves 2
Preparation time: 30 mins
Cooking time: 16 mins

Ingredients
300g (10½ oz) short-grain white rice

1 Wash the rice thoroughly in a strainer. Soak it in plenty of water for 30 minutes, then drain.

2 Place the rice in a pan with 300ml (10 fl oz) of water over a high heat and cover. When it comes to the boil, reduce the heat to low and cook for 8 minutes.

3 Remove from the heat and leave for 8 minutes without removing the lid.

4 Remove the lid and mix the rice thoroughly to separate the grains.

KATSUO DASHI
Basic dashi

Also known as katsuobushi, this common stock uses a combination of bonito (katsuo) flakes and kombu to produce a rich seafood flavour.

This recipe comes from Yoshihiro Murata, chef and owner of Kikunoi in Tokyo.

Makes 1.8 litres (3 pints)
Preparation time: 5 mins
Cooking time: 1 hr 30 mins

Ingredients
30g (1 oz) kombu
50g (13/4 oz) katsuobushi (dried bonito flakes)

1   Wipe the surface of the kombu with a damp tea towel and place in a large stockpot along with 1.8 litres (3 pints) of water. Place over low heat to bring the water up to 60°C/140°F (use a thermometer). Once the temperature has stabilised, leave to sit for 1 hour.

2   Remove the kombu using a slotted spoon and increase the heat to bring the stock up to 80°C/175°F. Be careful not to allow the stock to boil. Turn off the heat and immediately add the katsuobushi.

3   Leave the katsuobushi to soak for 10 seconds, then strain the stock through a fine sieve lined with muslin. The dashi will keep for a few days in the fridge.

KOMBU DASHI
Kelp dashi

A simple stock without the depth of flavour of katsuo dashi, kombu dashi is a good vegetarian alternative to use as a base for many Japanese dishes.

Adding one or two good-quality dried shiitake mushrooms can add richness to the stock.

Makes 500ml (17 fl oz)
Preparation time: 1–6 hrs
Cooking time: 10 mins

Ingredients
4cm² (½ sq inch) kombu

1   Add kombu to 500ml cold water and leave to steep for between an hour and half a day (depending on how strong a flavour you'd like).

2   Place on a high heat, removing the kombu just before the stock boils. Allow to cool. The dashi will keep for a few days in the fridge.

RECIPE SOURCES

NORTHERN JAPAN

① **Sumago Kudo**, Tsugaru Akatsuki Club, 39-7 Kamikonakano, Noheji, Kamikita District, Aomori (p12–15)

② **Ritsu and Keisuke Matsuura**, Matsuura Shokudo; 39–7 Kamikonakano, Noheji, Kamikita, Aomori (p16–19)

③ **Endo Kazunori and Kawakami Noriko**, Suzuki Shokudo, 32 Nosappu, Nemuro, Hokkaido (p20–23)

④ **Noriko Kudo**, Sanohe Nosankako Tomo no Kai, San Sun Chokubai Hiroba, 30–7 Nishihariwatashi, Kawamorita, Sannohe-machi, Sannohe-gun, Aomori (p24–7)

⑤ **Oku Masuhiko**, Menya Saimi, 5–3–12, 10–Jo Misono, Toyohira-ku, Sapporo, Hokkaido (p28–33)

⑥ **Nakamura Yasunori**, Kikuyo Shokudo, 11–15 Wakamatsu-cho, Hakodate, Hokkaido (p36–9)

⑦ **Hatsuo Sano**, Umami Tasuke, 2–11–11 Kokubuncho, Sendai (p40–43)

⑧ **Haruki Sato**, Mori-no-ie, 2052–1 Osawa, Mamurogawa, Mogami, Yamagata (p44–7)

⑨ **Kaneshika Sumiko**, Daurma Honten, 4 Minami 5–jo Nishi, Chuo-ku, Sapporo, Hokkaido (p48–51)

⑩ **Hiromi Ishida**, home cook, Rausu, Hokkaido (p52–5)

⑪ **Hiromi Hosoya**, Endo Mochiten, 4-7-26 Miyamachi, Aoba-ku, Sendai

TOKYO & CENTRAL JAPAN

① **Zaiyu Hasegawa**, Jimbocho Den, 2–2–å32 Jimbocho, Kanda, Chiyoda-ku, Tokyo www.jimbochoden.com (p62–5)

② **Fumio Kondo**, Tempura Kondo, 9th fl, Sakaguchi Building, 5–5–13 Ginza, Chuo-ku, Tokyo (p66–9)

③ **Ben Flatt**, Chikako Funashita, Flatts Inn, 27–26–3 Yanami, Noto-Chou, Ishikawa Prefecture flatt.jp (p70–73)

④ **Ryuichi Yui, Kizushi**, 2–7–13 Nihombashi Ningyocho, Chuo-ku, Tokyo (p74–7)

⑤ **Yosuke Miura**, Onigiri Asakusa Yadoroku, 3–9–10 Asakusa, Taito-ku, Tokyo onigiriyadoroku.com (p78–81)

⑥ **Akihiko Kadowaki**, Marunaka Lodge, 4424–2 Toyosato, Nozawa Onsen Village, Nagano (p82–5)

⑦ **Haruko**, Nobuko and Tsuguji Kitahira, Busuitei, 3–8–1 Mukaimachi, Furukawa, Hida, Gifu (p86–9)

⑧ **Tomoe Yoshikawa**, Sanyasou, Zenko Temple Entrance, 518 Daimon, Nagano Prefecture (p90–93)

⑨ **Yumi Chiba**, Anago Uotake Sushi, 122 Kusanago, Shimizu, Shizuoka (p94–9)

⑩ **Kouichi Tanaka**, Oyado Tanaka, 22–38 Kawaimachi, Wajima, Ishikawa Prefecture www.oyado-tanaka.jp (p100–103)

⑪ **Izuhi Yoshihara**, Tonki, 1–1–2 Shimo-Meguro, Meguro-ku, Tokyo (p104–7)

⑫ **Shinobu Namae**, L'Effervescence, 2–26–4 Nishi-azabu, Minato-ku Tokyo www.leffervescence.jp (p108–111)

⑬ **Hiroyasu Kayama**, Bar Ben Fiddich, 9F Yamatoya Bldg, 1–13–7 Nishi-Shinjuku, Shinjuku-ku, Tokyo (p112–5)

⑭ **Kouichiro Kawasaki**, Marukawa Miso, 12–62 Sugisaki-cho, Echizen-shi, Fukui marukawamiso.com (p116–9)

⑮ **Kazuo Kikuchi**, Wajindo, 2–10–6 Nakaimaizumi, Utsunomiya, Tochigi

KANSAI

① **Masaru Endo**, Aizu-ya, Chome-3-1 Tamadenishi, Nishinari Ward, Osaka www.aiduya.com (p126–9)

② **Katsumi Tanaka**, Konoha, 2 Chome-6-22 Minamihonmachi, Chūō, Osaka (p140–143)

③ **Imaki Takako**, Wasabi, Chome-1-17 Nanba, Chūō-ku, Osaka hozenji-wasabi.jp/ (p134–7)

④ **Masato Masuyama**, Kintame, 576 Botanbokocho, Kamigyo Ward, Kyoto www.kintame.co.jp (p138–141)

⑤ **Shuichi Neya**, Mimiu, 5-1-18 Nanba, Chuo Ward, Osaka (p142–5)

⑥ **Masahiro**, Grill Miyako, 650-0022 Hyōgo-ken, Kōbe grillmiyako.intrest. biz (p148–151)

7 **Taro Mishima**, Mishima-Tei, 405 Sakuranocho, Nakagyo Ward, Kyoto www.mishima-tei.co.jp (p152–5)

8 **Sousuke Hirai**, Hirasou, 614 Iigai, Yoshino, Nara (p156–9)

9 **Yanagimoto Yuki**, Awajiya, 3 Chome-6-18 Uozaki Minamimachi, Higashinada, Kōbe www.awajiya.co.jp (p160–163)

10 **Higaki Tomoaki,** Higaki, Nakayamatedori, Chuo Ward, Kobe (p164–7)

11 **Okamoto Masu**, Owariya, Kyoto honke-owariya.co.jp (p168–171)

12 **Kazuo Takagi**, Kyo-Ryori Takagi, 2-8 Ōharachō, Ashiya, Hyōgo www.kyotakagi.jp (p172–5)

13 **Shuichiro Kohori,** Fuka, 413 Higashi Uratsuji-Cho, Kyoto (p176–9)

14 **Hamano Koji** ,Kagizen Ryobo, 264 Gionmachi Kitagawa, Higashiyama, Kyōto www.kagizen.co.jp (p180–3)

WESTERN JAPAN

1 **Manabu Uekawa**, Mitchan, 730-0034, Hiroshima-ken, Hiroshima www.okonomi.co.jp (p186–9)

2 **Mr Ueno**, Ueno, 1-5-11 Miyajimaguchi, Hiroshima (p190–193)

3 **Shinichi Yamakoshi,** Yamago Udon, 61-2207Ayagawa-cho, 602-2 Hayukakami, Kagawa http://yamagoeudon.com (p196–9)

4 **Satoe Kishi**, Yamaai farm stay, Kamikatsu, Tokushima Prefecture www.kamikatsu.jp (p200–203)

5 **Toshihiro Hamada**, Hamagiku, 2 Chome-15-2, Kagoyamachi, Tokushima Prefecture (p204–7)

6 **Seiji Iwata**, Gansui, branches in Uwajima and Matsushima www.gansui.jp (p208–211)

7 **Kazuko Fukushima**, Fukuya, 1 Chome-2-22 Shōwachō, Kan'onji City, Kagawa www.niji.or.jp/home/fukuya/ (p212–5)

SOUTHERN JAPAN

1 **Kawashima Yoshimasa**, Kawashima Tofu, 1775 Kyomachi, Karatsu, Saga Prefecture zarudoufu.co.jp (p218–221)

2 **Saito Junya**, Ippudo Daimyo Honten, Fukuoka City, Fukuoka Prefecture (p222–5)

3 **Kawashima Rikio,** Kappo Hisago, Takezaki Town, Saga Prefecture (p228–31)

4 **Hiroyasu Tamaki**, Itoman Gyomin Shokudo,Naha (p232–5)

5 **Akio Yamashita**, Brazil Shokudo, 1703-6 Umusa, Nago-shi, Okinawa (p236–9)

6 **Masayasu Okouchi,** Yoyokaku, 2 Chome-4-40 Higashikaratsu, Karatsu-shi, Saga www.yoyokaku.com (p240–3)

7 **Tsutomu Motoyoshi**, Ganso Motoyoshiya, 69 Asahimachi, Yanagawa www.yanagawa-cci.or.jp (p244–7)

8 **Akinori Yashima**, Hachi-Bei, Fukuoka www.hachibei.com (p248–51)

9 **Hirokatsu Okutsu**, Toriden, Fukuoka www.toriden.com (p252–5)

10 **Karen**, 3-12 Yamanokuchichō, Kagoshima www.karen-ja.com (p256–9)

11 **Kakazu Zentaro,** Sashimitei, 882-7 Ōhama, Okinawa

BASIC RECIPES

Soranone Shokudou, on the shores of Lake Biwa (p264)

Yoshihiro Murata, Kikunoi, 6 Chome-13-8 Akasaka, Minato, Tokyo (p265)

GLOSSARY

hōjicha
Green tea with a mild, caramel-like flavour, usually made from bancha. Unlike other Japanese green teas the leaves are roasted, not steamed.

katakuriko
Fine potato starch used as a thickener for sauces or a crispy coating when frying. It is a gluten-free alternative to wheat flour.

katsuobushi
Dried, fermented and smoked skipjack tuna, though bonito is sometimes used as a cheaper alternative. Flakes are shaved from the dried fish. Has a smoky, savoury flavour.

miso paste
Traditional seasoning produced from fermented soybeans. The thick paste is used for sauces, spreads and soups.

niboshi
Dried baby sardines, used as a seasoning for stock or simply as a snack. The smaller ones have a milder flavour.

kombu
Edible kelp. Kombu is the only seaweed that can be used to make stock.

togarashi
Red chilli peppers. Also used as the general name for a group of condiments blending the peppers with other ingredients, notably shichimi.

ichimi red pepper seasoning
Ground dried red chilli peppers.

ikura
Large, reddish-orange salmon roe.

takuan
Pickled, sun-dried daikon radish. Thinly sliced, it is eaten as a side dish but also a snack.

kampyo
Dried shavings of *calabash*, a type of gourd. Commonly used as an ingredient in rolled sushi.

block konnyaku (taro cake)
Gelatinous preparation made from the pounded roots of the yam-like konjac plant, sold in 'cake' form. Has little flavour in itself but absorbs flavours from other ingredients. Used to add texture, and is noted for being filling and high in fibre with very few calories.

mochi
Short-grain japonica rice pounded into a paste and reshaped into a cake. It is used in many traditional Japanese sweets and is consumed widely at new year.

sansho
Common spice, also known as the Japanese pepper. Along with togarashi it is a key ingredient of shichimi.

kuzu
Arrowroot, source of the starch kuzuko. Used as a thickener in sauces and desserts, and can be used as a natural, unprocessed alternative to cornstarch. Gluten-free.

kinako
Literally 'yellow flour'. Flour made from roasted soybeans. A common ingredient noted for its sweet flavour and powdery texture. It is not as sweet as sugar, but is still used in desserts.

tobiko
Roe of the flying fish, commonly used in sushi. It has a mild smoky or salty flavour.

konka saba
Fermented mackerel made by packing the fish with fermented rice bran, sliced red chillies and salt, and leaving for a year or two.

nori seaweed
Edible seaweed commonly used as a wrap for sushi, but also as a garnish or flavouring in noodles and soups.

tsukudani paste
Black paste commonly made from roasted nori seaweed and used as a salty condiment.

yomogi
Leaves of the Japanese mugwort plant, sometimes blanched and added to soups, rice or even sweets.

konnyaku (shirataki) noodles
Literally 'white waterfall'. Translucent noodles made from the konjac yam.

ABOUT THE WRITERS

Tienlon Ho first backpacked around Japan in 2001, powered by ramen, onigiri, and vending machine milk tea. She has returned many times since to write about food and travel for Lonely Planet and other publications. Read more at tienlon.com and @tienlonho.

My gratitude goes to Ayako Mochimaru, who assisted with this project with grace and ingenuity.

Rebecca Milner: California-raised, product of Tokyo since 2002. Rebecca has travelled the breadth and length of Japan as an author for Lonely Planet and just for fun, always following up on tips from friends of what to eat and where. She is also a former dining columnist for the *Japan Times*.

Thank you to Jess for her leap of faith and patience. To photographer Junichi for driving us all over Tohoku & Hokkaido, setting up interviews and, most importantly, not hitting the deer. To all the chefs who let us into their kitchens and gave generously of their time and secrets. To Ippo for teaching me much about Japanese food over the years; to Tienlon for her tips and ideas; to Kobayashi-san for his Aomori contacts. And to my husband and friends in Tokyo who helped me road test the recipes.

Ippo Nakahara is a journalist born in Saga Prefecture in 1977. After graduating from high school, he began writing about food while working on a food stall in Fukuoka. His work focuses on food itself, human nature and life stories told through food. He has published his essays through magazine, TV and radio.

ABOUT THE PHOTOGRAPHER

Junichi Miyazaki believes that food photography is similar to portraiture: when we see a photograph of a dish of food, what we're really seeing is the chef who created it, in the same way that when we stand in a field of crops, we learn about the farmer who planted them. Shooting the food, places and chefs for these pages, Junichi's aim was to convey the full context of each regional cuisine, and to tell the story behind each dish. www.junichimiyazaki.com

INDEX

Published in September 2016 by Lonely Planet Global Limited
CRN 554153
www.lonelyplanet.com
ISBN 978 1 76034 298 2
© Lonely Planet 2016
Printed in China

Written by Tienlon Ho (Tokyo & Central Japan); Rebecca Milner (Northern Japan, plus features on *tomorokoshi tempura* and *ichigo kakigori*) and Ippo Nakahara (Kansai, Western Japan and Southern Japan)

Managing Director, Publishing Piers Pickard
Associate Publisher Robin Barton
Commissioning Editor Jessica Cole
Editors Kate Wanwimolruk and Claire Naylor
Art Direction Daniel Di Paolo
Layout Designer Lauren Egan
Illustrator Louise Sheeran
Cartographers Wayne Murphy, Corey Hutchison
Print Production Larissa Frost, Nigel Longuet

Thanks to Laura Crawford, Jonathan Eyers, Masae Ito, Meri Joyce, Matt Phillips, Ken Rhodes

With thanks to the recipe testers Britney Alvarez, Tim Burland, Dan Di Paolo, Amy Lysen, Matt Hardy, Cate Jacques, Thom Shaw, Luna Soo, Emma Totney, Tracy Whitmey

All photographs by Junichi Miyazaki

Lonely Planet offices

AUSTRALIA
The Malt Store, Level 3, 551 Swanston Street, Carlton VIC, 3053 Australia
Phone 03 8379 8000

USA
150 Linden St, Oakland, CA 94607
Phone 510 250 6400

UNITED KINGDOM
240 Blackfriars Road, London SE1 8NW
Phone 020 3771 5100

IRELAND
Unit E, Digital Court, The Digital Hub, Rainsford St, Dublin 8

STAY IN TOUCH lonelyplanet.com/contact

Paper in this book is certified against the Forest Stewardship Council™ standards. FSC™ promotes environmentally responsible, socially beneficial and economically viable management of the world's forests.